In Miami Beach's Art Deco District

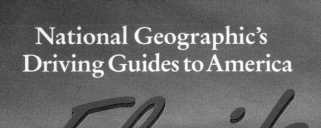

National Geographic's
Driving Guides to America

Florida
And Alabama, Georgia, South Carolina, North Carolina, Tennessee, and Kentucky

By John M. Thompson
Photographed by Raymond Gehman

Prepared by
The Book Division
National Geographic Society
Washington, D.C.

Credits

National Geographic's Driving Guides To America Florida and the Southeast

By JOHN M. THOMPSON
Photographed by RAYMOND GEHMAN

Published by
THE NATIONAL GEOGRAPHIC SOCIETY

Reg Murphy
President and Chief Executive Officer
Gilbert M. Grosvenor
Chairman of the Board
Nina D. Hoffman
Senior Vice President

Prepared by The Book Division

William R. Gray
Vice President and Director
Charles Kogod
Assistant Director
Barbara A. Payne
Editorial Director and Managing Editor

Driving Guides to America

Elizabeth L. Newhouse
Director of Travel Publishing and Series Editor
Cinda Rose
Art Director
Thomas B. Powell III
Illustrations Editor
Caroline Hickey, Barbara A. Noe
Senior Researchers
Carl Mehler
Map Editor and Designer

Staff for this book

Caroline Hickey
Project Manager
K. M. Kostyal
Text Editor
Joan Wolbier
Designer
Thomas B. Powell III
Illustrations Editor

Carl Mehler
Map Editor and Designer

Mark T. Fitzgerald
Sean M. Groom
Michael H. Higgins
Mary E. Jennings
Keith R. Moore
Shana E. Vickers
Researchers

Barbara A. Noe
Contributing Editor

Paulette L. Claus
Editorial Consultant

Tracey M. Wood
Map Production Manager
Sven M. Dolling, Thomas L. Gray, Joseph F. Ochlak, Tracey M. Wood
Map Research
Sven M. Dolling, Louis J. Spirito
Map Production
Tibor G. Tóth
Map Relief

Meredith C. Wilcox
Illustrations Assistant

Richard S. Wain
Production Project Manager
Lewis R. Bassford, Lyle Rosbotham
Production

Kevin G. Craig, Dale M. Herring, Peggy J. Purdy
Staff Assistants

Susan Fels
Indexer

Thomas B. Blabey
Contributor

Manufacturing and Quality Management

George V. White, *Director*
John T. Dunn, *Associate Director*
Vincent P. Ryan, *Manager*

Cover: Along US 1, Florida Keys
BRUCE DALE

Previous pages: Skylift above Main Street Pier, Daytona Beach, Florida

Facing page: Cumberland Gap National Historical Park, Kentucky, Tennessee, Virginia

Library of Congress CIP data: page 160

Plains, Georgia, water tower

4

Contents

6

$\mathcal{S}$omewhere in my father's bureau is a minié ball handed down from my great-grandfather. He was shot in the neck during Pickett's Charge at Gettysburg and sat out the rest of the war in a Union prison camp with that ball lodged under his tongue. Like my ancestors for more than 200 years, I grew up in North Carolina's Piedmont. Spending Sunday afternoons listening to the stories of Miss Myrtle and Mama Joyce, my grandmothers, was something I took for granted. My family vacationed on Pawleys Island, South Carolina, a languid strand of palmettos, mellow voices, and cottages once owned by wealthy planters. As with many other southern families, we had these relics, stories, and places that attached us to a history larger than our own. But the South was just home, and years would go by before I would begin to appreciate what it was all about.

Kentucky Horse Park, Lexington

8

For one thing, it's about the past and longing for the past—not necessarily for better times, but simply for times gone and unrecoverable. The South has the most highly developed sense of history of any region in the country—a complex of pride and shame and repressed memory. You'll feel these mixed emotions especially at the surviving plantations. Shrouded by ancient moss-laden trees, these places of unspeakable beauty steadfastly guard the flame of southern heritage. And you'll feel it at Civil War sites that mark the land all the way to Key West, for the war is the time line pivot from which all southern history is measured.

Then there's the strong southern sense of place, a reverence for landscapes in their wondrous variety—rolling blue mountains, sandy beaches, turquoise coral reefs. Not to mention horse farms greener than new money, old coastal cities, small-town cafés, and marshes so golden at sunset that you want to stay forever. And you'll find a host of people anxious to tell the history of these places, in melodic voices ranging from rural banjo twang to aristocratic broad to soft Gulla.

As you travel, remember that behind every fancy New South facade there's an Old South story. Until there comes an event to outdo—or undo—the Civil War, that will never change. As novelist William Faulkner expressed it, "The past is never dead, it isn't even past."

JOHN M. THOMPSON

Traveling Easy

Traveling the South is almost always easy. Roads are kept in good condition, and weather is generally not an issue, with a few exceptions: The upper states do have a winter, especially in the mountains where you can find yourself in a sudden brief snowstorm. And along the coast in summer, hurricanes can be a problem. In general fall is a wonderful time in the Southeast, with lots of colorful foliage and few crowds. Spring is highly popular with azalea and camellia lovers, while the infamous heat and humidity of summer are mostly overrated. After all, summer will always be a great time to take to the road.

*N*ATIONAL GEOGRAPHIC'S DRIVING GUIDES TO AMERICA invite you on memorable road trips through the United States and Canada. Intended both as travel planners and companions, each volume guides you on preplanned tours over a wide variety of terrain to the best places to see and things to do. The authors, expert regional travel writers, star-rate (from none to two ★★) the drives and points of interest to make sure you don't miss their favorites.

All distances and drive times are approximate (if you linger, as you should, plan on considerably more time). Recommended seasons are the best times to go, but roads and sites are open all year unless otherwise noted. Besides the stated days of operation, many sites close on national holidays. For the most up-to-date site information, it's best to call ahead when possible.

Then, with this book and a road map, set off on your adventure through this awesomely beautiful land.

Magnolia Plantation, near Charleston, S.C.

9

MAP KEY and ABBREVIATIONS

Military Reservation	
National Estuarine Research Reserve	N.E.R.R
National Historical Park	N.H.P.
National Monument	NAT. MON., N.M.
National Park	N.P.
National Preserve	
National Recreation Area	N.R.A.
National River and Recreation Area	
National Seashore	
Naval Air Station	
National Forest	NAT. FOR., N.F.
National Wildlife Refuge	N.W.R.
National Key Deer Refuge	
State Natural Area	
State Park	S.P.
State Recreation Park	
State Resort Park	S.R.P.
Indian Reservation	IND. RES., I.R.

Featured Drive

Interstate Highway
(95)

U.S. Federal Highway
(80)

State Road
(30)

County, Local, or Other Road
[318]

Ferry
FEATURED   OTHER

State Border

Canal

Boundaries

NAT. FOREST   NAT. PARK/ NAT. PRESERVE

■ Point of Interest
⊛ State Capital
| Dam
+ Elevation, Peak
= Falls

Swamp

ADDITIONAL ABBREVIATIONS

FT.	*Fort*
HWY.	*Highway*
L.	*Lake*
MEM.	*Memorial*
Mt.-s.	*Mount-ain-s*
NAT.	*National*
NAT. MEM.	*National Memorial*
N.B.	*National Battlefield*
N.B.P.	*National Battlefield Park*
N.H.S.	*National Historic Site*
N.M.P.	*National Military Park*
PKWY.	*Parkway*
R.	*River*
S.C.P.	*State Conservation Park*
S.H.A.	*State Historic Area*
S.H.P.	*State Historic-al Park*
S.H.S.	*State Historic Site*
S.R.A.	*State Recreation Area*

POPULATION

● **Memphis**	500,000 and over
● **Augusta**	50,000 to under 500,000
● Hatteras	under 50,000

Forgotten Florida

● **360 miles** ● **3 to 4 days** ● **Year-round**

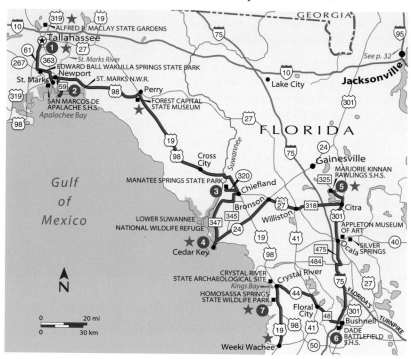

See p. 32

An easygoing cruise down the long underbelly of the Florida peninsula hearkens back to an older, simpler Sunshine State. This quieter coast with a slower pace preserves tourism 1950s style and what Floridians consider the "real Florida." Entertainment is as enchanting as a glass-bottom boat ride over crystal-clear springs and rarely more sophisticated than a mermaid performance or trained parrot show.

Starting in the heart of Florida's Dixie, the drive visits the capital of Tallahassee before dropping south to a lovely state park, a 17th-century Spanish fort, and a national wildlife refuge. Then curving southeast, the route explores peaceful wetlands and mangrove-fringed shores. An excursion inland crosses citrus country and the haunt of writer Marjorie Kinnan Rawlings; Ocala offers good museums and one of the area's many natural-springs theme parks. Heading west again, you enter a land of alligators and manatees, pine hammocks and still more springs.

Old Capitol, Tallahassee

Tucked into the gentle hills near the Georgia border,
❶ **Tallahassee**★ *(Visitor Center, Florida State Capitol, S. Duval St. 904-413-9200)* was an 1820s compromise location between the former capitals of Pensacola and St. Augus-

St. Marks National Wildlife Refuge

tine. Take a look at the land from the 22nd floor of the **Florida State Capitol**★ *(904-488-6167)*. Beyond the city, nothing but forests stretch as far as the eye can see.

While here, walk to the adjacent **Old Capitol**★ *(Monroe St. and Apalachee Pkwy. 904-487-1902)*, distinguished by its handsome Greek Revival portico and candy-striped awnings that re-create the way it would have appeared in 1902. Inside, restored areas include the rotunda, the governor's private suite, the supreme court, and the house and senate chambers.

Two blocks west the **Museum of Florida History**★ *(500 S. Bronough St. 904-488-1484)* houses an overwhelming hodgepodge of stuff that includes a 12,000-year-old mastodon skeleton found in nearby Wakulla Springs; Spanish galleon booty; and a re-creation of early tourist camps.

For a fascinating look at an active archaeological dig, drive over to the **San Luis Archaeological and Historic Site**★ *(2020 W. Mission Rd. 904-487-3711)*, where Spanish friars set up a mission village in 1656 and lived among the resident Apalachee Indians. Self-guided tours cover the fort and church sites and a council house excavation.

North of Tallahassee is the **Alfred B. Maclay State Gardens**★ *(US 319. 904-487-4556. Adm. fee)*, a highly

Forgotten Florida

recommended attraction bursting with camellias, azaleas, and more than 160 other species of flowering shrubs. You stroll the wooded and formal areas on soft grass or pine needle paths and breathe in beauty and serenity. For the best effect, sit on the bench in the walled garden and look through the arched wall and down a long, palm-lined vista to a reflecting pool and distant Lake Hall—you'll almost feel like you're in a landscape painting.

Head south on Fla. 61 and stop at **Edward Ball Wakulla Springs State Park** (*Fla. 267 and Fla. 61. 904-922-3632. Adm. fee*), a 3,000-acre preserve centering around one of several springs in the state touted as Juan Ponce de León's fountain of youth. The 1937 lodge has an impressive lobby with painted cypress beams and a massive fireplace; the restaurant offers simple, wholesome fare. If you take a glass-bottom boat trip you're likely to see gators, turtles, a number of graceful birds, and a clientele that predates the lodge. There's nothing overly exciting about this antiquated, friendly attraction, which is exactly its appeal.

Continue south on Fla. 363 to **St. Marks,** a tousled little wharf town with a couple of seafood restaurants and a fishing camp. The point of land where the St. Marks and Wakulla Rivers meet quietly and flow to the Gulf first attracted military attention more than 300 years ago. At the **San Marcos de Apalache State Historic Site** (*1 mile SW of Fla. 363 on Old Fort Rd.; follow signs. 904-925-6216. Thurs.-Mon.; adm. fee for museum*), you can see the remains of Spanish and Confederate forts; an informative museum holds unearthed artifacts.

Head northeast and east on US 98 to Newport, then south on County Rd. 59 to **❷ St. Marks National Wildlife Refuge** (*904-925-6121. Adm. fee*), a vast tract on Apalachee Bay. The Visitor Center has exhibits, a 15-minute film, and a nice little interpretive trail around a murky pond. You can also take the 7-mile road down to an 1829 lighthouse and adjacent observation tower still in use today.

East on US 98 sends you down a long, lonely piece of highway, where in 40 miles there's only one gas station. Along here fluffy pampas grass waves behind screens of trees, and a bear-habitat sign is about the only indication of higher life. Quite a bit of forestry goes on in these woods, but you still have the sense you're visiting an area few people know about.

In **Perry** (*Chamber of Commerce 904-584-5366*), you'll find out more about the forest industry at the **Forest Capital State Museum** ★ (*1 mile S on US 98. 904-584-3227.*

Thurs.-Mon.; adm. fee), a building redolent of cypress and cedar. Display cases, each made from a different native wood, show the importance of Florida's third largest business. Included are exhibits on turpentine, virgin forests, and the sex life of a pine tree. Out back, surrounded by woods, an 1864 homestead of weathered boards gives a feeling for what it was like to light a candle in the wilderness.

Continue south on US 19 through the sparsely populated Big Bend area. Detours to the Gulf lead to untrafficked coastal villages hit hard by the recent ban on net fishing. Entrepreneurs are diversifying into ecotourism. To sample some of this product, go west on Fla. 320, just outside Chiefland. At ❸ **Manatee Springs State Park** *(352-493-6072. Adm. fee)*, you can swim in the clear-as-glass headwaters of a first magnitude spring. Also in this delightful park, a short boardwalk trail ventures into a cypress swamp, ending at the Suwannee River.

From Chiefland, head south on County Rd. 345, then take County Rd. 347 west a few miles to the **Lower Suwannee National Wildlife Refuge** *(352-493-0238)*. Hiking and driving trails in the 51,000-acre preserve almost guarantee a look at alligators and shorebirds.

Now continue south on County Rd. 347 and Fla. 24 across a series of bridges that link gorgeous islands rimmed by marshes and sun-spangled waters. ❹ **Cedar Key**★, an island town that is still prospering, feels like a Key West from the past. A no-frills resort, it has the same ends-of-the-earth feel and stunning sunsets. Stop in the **Cedar Key Historical Society Museum** *(Fla. 24 and 2nd St. 352-543-5549. Adm. fee)*, an 1871 house that offers a vest-pocket overview of local history. Exhibits tell the Cedar Key story from blockade-running during the Civil War to timber harvesting to the 1896 hurricane that wiped the town out.

Marjorie Kinnan Rawlings State Historic Site

Head inland on Fla. 24 to Bronson, then take US 27A to Williston and County Rd. 318 east to Citra. You're now in the rural South again, a land of rolling farms and cattle clustered in the gauzy shade of big live oaks. This is the heart of citrus country, so stop at a roadside stand for fresh oranges and juice, then go north on US 301 and County Rd. 325. Beside the county park, the

Crystal River State Archaeological Site

⑤ Marjorie Kinnan Rawlings State Historic Site★ *(352-466-3672. Grounds daily, house tours Oct.-July. Thurs.-Sun.; adm. fee to house)* was the house where the author wrote her 1938 classic, *The Yearling,* and other books. She chose the rambling one-story farmhouse with its citrus grove and pastureland as an "escape from urban confusion," which it still more or less is. A typewriter like the one she used sits out on a side porch, and an open suitcase lies half packed in the bedroom, as though she'd just returned from a trip.

Take US 301 south to **Ocala** *(Chamber of Commerce 352-629-8051)* and make a pilgrimage to **Silver Springs** *(Fla. 40. 352- 236-2121. Adm. fee),* one of the oldest tourist attractions in the state and the first to use glass-bottom tour boats. Since 1878, visitors have been coming to this nature park to behold its crystalline waters and exotic flora. Billed as the world's largest artesian spring, the system is actually composed of about 150 springs that together gush 5,000 gallons of pure water a second. To get your money's worth, you need to take a glass-bottom boat ride and a Jeep safari into a 35-acre habitat housing animals from around the globe.

Backtrack 2 miles to the **Appleton Museum of Art★** *(4533 N.E. Silver Springs Blvd. 352-236-7100. Closed Mon.; adm. fee),* which presents an eclectic display of Asian antiquities, pre-Columbian art, Columbian pottery, African totems, European decorative arts, and works by minor painters. The building itself, with its bright breezeways and large windows, perhaps outdoes the collection in aesthetic appeal.

Arthur Appleton, whose 1986 donation built the museum, owns one of the county's 400 horse farms. Take

County Rd. 475 (Third Avenue) or County Rd. 475A (27th Street) south to see a countryside littered with gloriously ritzy training and breeding facilities for Thoroughbreds, Arabians, Paso Finos, and other breeds.

Go south on I-75 to County Rd. 48, heading east toward Bushnell. Follow signs to ❻ **Dade Battlefield State Historic Site** *(W of US 301. 352-793-4781. Adm. fee)*, scene of a bloody episode on Dec. 28, 1835. That morning, as 108 soldiers marched through woods and fields toward Fort King, near Ocala, a larger number of Seminole ambushed them, killing all but two. Resisting their removal to Oklahoma, the Indians sparked the long and costly Second Seminole War. Today, popular reenactments the first weekend in January recall the horrors of the battle.

Head back west on County Rd. 48 to Floral City, a faded flower from the turn of the century, then take US 41 to Fla. 44. This will bring you to **Crystal River** *(Chamber of Commerce, 28 N.W. Hwy. 19. 352-795-3149. Mon.-Fri.)*, one of the state's largest manatee wintering grounds. The chance to spot these rare sea cows—about 200 migrate to Kings Bay between January and March— makes scuba diving and snorkeling two of the area's most popular sports. To learn about the earliest humans here, follow signs 3 miles west to **Crystal River State Archaeological Site** *(3400 N. Museum Pt. 352-795-3817. Adm. fee)*, where Native American middens (trash mounds), burial mounds, and temple mounds date from 200 B.C. to A.D. 1400. A half-mile trail leads past mounds and ceremonial stones; the Visitor Center has a good video and displays.

About 7 miles south on US 19/98 (Suncoast Blvd.), watch for the entrance to ❼ **Homosassa Springs State Wildlife Park**★ *(352-628-2311. Adm. fee)*, centered around a 45-foot-deep spring. If you come in the main entrance, you'll have to take a boat trip along Pepper Creek to get to the park. Once there, you can walk nature trails past orphaned and injured bears, an endangered Florida panther, bobcats, and other native wildlife. An underwater observatory gives you close-up views of manatees, many injured by boats and awaiting release back to the wild.

Weeki Wachee theme park

Continue down US 19 to **Weeki Wachee**★ *(US 19 and Fla. 50. 352-596-2062. Adm. fee)*, a haven for earnest kitsch since 1946. The theme park offers a river cruise, an exotic bird show, a petting zoo, and acrobatic macaws. But what everyone comes for is the mermaid show. An underwater window gives a wide view of the proceedings.

US 19 and US 27 will take you back to Tallahassee.

Tampa Bay Circle ★

● **160 miles** ● **3 days** ● **Year-round**

The greatest population center on Florida's west coast, Tampa Bay has a serious side and a fun side. This mostly urban loop explores them both. As in Miami, geography gives only a rough sense of where the work area ends and the play area begins. True, the beaches are gorgeous and developed for tourism, but the city has an equal share of fun things to do. And though you'll visit some "historical" attractions, west Florida is history lite compared with the rest of the South—other than the land, there's hardly anything more than a hundred years old.

Beginning with a city tour of Tampa, you'll feast on art, modern architecture, and a brand-new aquarium. You then drive northwest to Tarpon Springs for a taste of Greek sponge-diving culture, and south along the coast through honky-tonk beach towns. With scenery varying from dull suburban strip to beautiful island shore, this drive never fails to deliver an interesting attraction right when you need it. After perusing the stellar cultural offerings of St. Petersburg, you cross Tampa Bay on the most spectacular bridge in the South—the 4.1-mile Sunshine Skyway. Down in no-nonsense Bradenton and artsy Sarasota, another spectrum of diversions awaits you, including a sublime palace of art built by circus impresario John Ringling.

In the past two decades, ❶ **Tampa**★ *(Visitor Center, 111 E. Madison St. 813-223-1111. Closed Sun.)* has fountained from a town of bland warehouses and office buildings into a zesty city of 40-story skyscrapers. Walking the not-bad pedestrian mall on Franklin Street, you'll see examples of restored old buildings alongside spanking new ones. The city got its real start in 1890 when Henry Plant brought his railroad here and built the fabulous Tampa Bay Hotel, now belonging to the University of Tampa and the **Henry B. Plant Museum**★ *(401 W. Kennedy Blvd. 813-254-1891. Closed Mon.; adm. fee).* Recognized by its gleaming crescent-topped minarets, the old hotel museum greets visitors with its wide porches and fancy fretwork. Low-level lighting and luxurious Victorian furnishings re-create the gilded age of Florida tourism. After

17

Tampa Bay and the Sunshine Skyway Bridge

watching a 14-minute video, you peek into the reading room, parlor suite, grand salon, and other rooms.

Construction continues down at the new Garrison Seaport, but the **Florida Aquarium**★★ *(701 Channelside Dr. 813-273-4000. Adm. fee)* is already open for business. Displaying 600 Florida species, this large and entertaining facility guides visitors through four aquatic communities: wetlands, bays and beaches, coral reefs, and offshore. The highlight of the aquarium, a 43-by-14-foot clear acrylic wall, offers marvelous views of tropical fish swimming through an artificial reef.

While the Plant Museum preserves tourist history, **Ybor** ("E-bore") **City**★, a mile from downtown, is a living (and lively) monument to the city's immigrant working class. Globe lamps, wrought-iron balconies, and decorative tilework have been spruced up or added to this cigarmaking neighborhood that flourished from the 1880s to 1920s, making Tampa synonymous with cigars. Reclaimed from urban decay, Ybor City—named after Vicente Ybor, a Cuban exile and cigar manufacturer—has turned into a youthful mélange of boutiques, restaurants, and nightclubs—gay and straight. You can once again buy hand-rolled cigars here, and lunch on Cuban sandwiches. The main action concentrates on Seventh Avenue.

Museum of Science and Industry

You can easily blow another half day turning the many levers and pressing the numerous buttons at the **Museum of Science and Industry**★ *(4801 E. Fowler Ave. 813-987-6300. Adm. fee)*, a gargantuan hands-on learning center that takes in two buildings and three floors. Don't miss the hurricane room and the tesla chamber, where you can discharge a 10,000-volt whip of lightning. And for a totally absorbing cinematic experience, watch a film in the domed MOSIMAX theater, equipped with seven-speaker digital sound and a 10,500-square-foot screen.

From Tampa, take Fla. 580 and County Rd. 752 west to US 19, then go north to ❷ **Tarpon Springs**★ *(Chamber of Commerce, 11 E. Orange St. 813-937-6109. Mon.-Fri.)*, a pocket of Greek culture since the first Aegean Islanders were recruited for their diving skills in 1905. The sponge industry almost died out in the 1940s but revived in the

Sponge boat, Tarpon Springs

'80s, and now Dodecanese Boulevard is a Mediterranean bazaar of bouzouki music, wind chimes tinkling in front of gift shops, and leathery old men hawking boat tours. You can stock up on sponges and loofahs, eat some souvlaki, and then watch a diving demonstration.

On a quiet side street, the **Universalist Church**★ (57 *Read St. 813-937-4682. Oct.-May Tues.-Sun.; adm. fee)* houses 11 large landscape paintings by George Inness, Jr., who in the early part of the century lived in nearby Inness Manor (34 W. Orange St. Private).

For some relief from urban sight-seeing, travel south on US 19A to Fla. 586, and take the causeway-drawbridge out to **Honeymoon Island State Park** (813 469 5912. Adm. fee). Promoted as a romantic getaway in the early 1940s, the barrier island is now mostly preserved parkland. From the beach there's a fine sweeping view of the Gulf of Mexico and the high hotels of Clearwater Beach far on the southern horizon. Though this shore tends to be rocky, a daily ferry (813-734-5263. Weather permitting; fare) takes visitors to a 3-mile sliver of brilliant white sand on adjacent **Caladesi Island State Park**★ (813-469-5918. Adm. fee), separated from Honeymoon Island by a 1921 hurricane.

Continuing south on US 19A, you come to **Clearwater** *(Chamber of Commerce, 1130 Cleveland St. 813-461-0011. Mon.-Fri.)*, a big vacation center due west of Tampa. You're now on the Pinellas Peninsula, about 15 miles at its widest and thoroughly planted with businesses and houses inland and motels and restaurants along its coast. Lined with royal and sabal palms, the Garden Memorial Causeway (Fla. 60) out to Clearwater Beach is your red-carpet reward for putting up with Clearwater's traffic. The bridge gives excellent views of the glimmering harbor and the condos and motels on the beach.

Turn south on Gulf Boulevard, and pass through the town of Clearwater Beach, where a half dozen cruise lines offer a variety of entertainment ranging from historical narrations to dinner dances and casinos. For quieter interludes with nature, try **Sand Key Park**★ (1060 Gulf Blvd. 813-595-7677)—a 95-acre playground of wide sandy beach.

Continue south through the next stretch of beach communities. Though fairly well built-up, the strip does offer plenty of beach access and occasional Gulf views, as well as many chances for buying T-shirts and other gifts. Just south of County Rd. 694, the ❸ **Suncoast Seabird Sanctuary** *(18328 Gulf Blvd. 813-391-6211)* annually treats some 5,000 pelicans, hawks, owls, herons, and other birds injured by fishing lines, cars, and other man-made obstacles. About

Land for Sale

The image of Florida as a hotbed of real estate chicanery stems from the 1920s, when the state was a speculator's dream, madness breeding insanity under a steamy subtropical sun. It was the decade when anyone with a feel for the value of hype could make a fortune overnight. A person literally could buy unimproved acreage, turn around and sell it within a few hours, and come out with a nice profit. One spectator neatly summed up the surreal frenzy: "A lie told in the morning can become true in the afternoon." Though the building boom collapsed in 1926, it left behind the great resorts and mansions in Palm Beach and Miami, and the luxury developments that filled in the swamps of the west coast.

19

60 percent survive, and most of these are returned to the wild. The others have a permanent home here. Sensing a safe place, several injured birds have walked right into the sanctuary off the beach.

Travel south on Gulf Boulevard along an area called the Suncoast and you eventually arrive in St. Pete Beach, unmistakably marked by the pink-stucco **Don CeSar Beach Resort** *(3400 Gulf Blvd. 813-360-1881)*. Built in 1928, the grand Moorish-style hotel hosted such luminaries as Franklin Roosevelt and F. Scott Fitzgerald. Reopened in 1973 after decades of decline, the Don shows off Cuban tile floors, Italian marble fountains, and crystal chandeliers.

Take the Pinellas Bayway (Fla. 682) east, and divert south on Fla. 679 about 7 miles to ❹ **Fort De Soto Park**★ *(3500 Pinellas Bayway S. 813-866-2484)*, on unspoiled Mullet Key. The sleepy fort was started in 1898 during the short-lived Spanish-American War, but never saw action and remained unfinished. Wander around the powder magazines and thick walls, then go fishing or stroll on a solitary beach within distant view of the crowd-happy Suncoast and the glittering Sunshine Skyway Bridge.

First pop up to ❺ **St. Petersburg**★ and drive to the **Salvador Dali Museum**★★ *(1000 3rd St. S. 813-823-3767. Adm. fee)*, one of the state's top cultural attractions. The world's

Salvador Dali Museum, St. Petersburg

most compre-hensive collection of Dali's works, the museum is arranged in chronological order (1914-80) to show the artist's development. The south wall alone is enough to convince anyone of Dali's genius—four breathtaking allegories (each about 13-by-10 feet) combine his historical and scientific obsessions with precise trompe l'oeil effects.

Dali would have enjoyed the nearby **Great Explorations**★ *(1120 4th St. S. 813-821-8885. Adm. fee)*, ranking as one of Florida's best children's museums, with 15,550 square feet of space for imaginative hands-on activities in science, art, and music.

The **Museum of Fine Arts**★ *(Beach Dr. and 2nd Ave. N.E. 813-896-2667. Closed Mon.; adm. fee)* holds a delightful collection of world art in 20 galleries. Represented here

are such masters as Monet, Renoir, O'Keeffe, and others.

By now you've noticed the inverted pyramid at the end of **The Pier** *(E end of 2nd Ave. N.E. 813-821-6164)*, which hops day and night with fishermen, Jet skiers, sailors, and putt-putt golfers. Enjoy some fresh fish with your bay view at the restaurant on the pyramid's top floor; also inside are an Information Center and aquarium.

Before leaving St. Petersburg, take a look downtown at the 1920s Mediterranean Revival architecture *(around 4th St. and Central Ave.)*. Reinforcing the time-capsule feel are nearby lawn bowling and shuffleboard clubs from the same era, as well as the **Coliseum** *(535 4th Ave. N. 813-892-5202)*, featured in the movie *Cocoon*, which still holds sock hops and tea dances.

South Florida Museum, Bradenton

Prepare for a sudden reentry into modern technology as you head south over the dazzling **Sunshine Skyway**★★ *(Toll)*, a 15-mile chain of causeways and bridges. Not for the acrophobic, the skyway features a 4-mile midsection soaring 183 feet above Tampa Bay and supported by a fan of bright yellow cables that look more like modern art than reliable engineering—they actually rise not on either side of the bridge, but single file in the median! A scenic view pull-off near the beginning helps drivers avoid the temptation to stare at the incomparable bay vistas.

Follow I-275 to I-75 south, and take the first exit (US 301) west about a mile to the **Gamble Plantation State Historic Site**★ *(941-723-4536. Thurs.-Mon.; adm. fee)*, a restored Greek Revival mansion that presided over a 3,500-acre sugar plantation. The 45-minute house tour provides keen insight into the life of south Florida's sole surviving antebellum plantation.

Drive on to ❻ **Bradenton** *(Visitor Center, 530 Hwy. 301 N. 941-729-7040)*, Sarasota's blue-collar brother, and stop off at the **South Florida Museum and Bishop Planetarium** *(201 10th St. W. 941-746-4131. Closed Mon.; adm. fee)*. This large and varied facility offers a little of everything—shells and minerals, reproduction pioneer rooms, a live manatee, and a planetarium presenting star and laser shows. Bradenton's historical claim to fame is quite significant and lies only a few miles west on Manatee Avenue (Fla. 64), and north on 75th Street West. The **De Soto National Memorial**★ *(941-792-0458)* commemorates the 1539 landing of Hernando de Soto's nine galleons. Standing here at the edge of Tampa Bay, you can try to imagine what a remarkable sight those ships must have been to the Native Americans. With an army of 600, the Spanish explorer set out on the first major exploration of North America (see sidebar, p. 12). The Visitor Center does a good job with both the expedition's boldness and its devastating effect on local culture.

Continue west on Fla. 64 across a causeway adorned with palms and pines. On Anna Maria Island, head south on Gulf of Mexico Drive (Fla. 789) through Bradenton Beach, a colorful little seaside town of 1950s-era motels and souvenir shops. At the island's south end, lovely **Coquina Beach** has picnic tables, a snack bar, a playground, and a wide swath of powdery sand edging the warm and welcoming Gulf waters.

Cross the inlet, slowing for a fine view of the ocean and Sarasota Bay, and you're on Longboat Key, a slender 10-mile island tastefully developed with lowlying houses and lush tropical landscaping that grows posher as you travel south. After the next inlet, turn left and visit the **Mote Marine Aquar-**

John and Mable Ringling Museum of Art, Sarasota

ium (1600 Ken Thompson Pkwy. 941-388-2451. Adm. fee), a nonprofit outfit that conducts research on sharks and environmental pollutants. Among the many aquariums here is a 135,000-gallon shark tank with above- and below-water viewing, and a touch tank where you can handle a sea urchin, a horseshoe crab, and other marine animals. Be sure to stop in at the **Pelican Man's Bird Sanctuary**★ (1708 Ken Thompson Pkwy. 941-388-4444), just down the road. Strolling the boardwalk past 50 squawking pens of injured birds gives you hope that this rapidly developing area has not gone completely out of control.

Drive down to **St. Armands Circle**★ (W end of Ringling Causeway/Fla. 789. 941-388-1554), the most glamorous shopping district on the west coast. Around the circle and its bisecting streets are a hundred high-end stores and restaurants. You'll have a hard time finding a plastic snow

bubble here, but you can buy ice cream or a sandwich and do some people-watching. John Ringling developed St. Armands in the 1920s, along with the Ringling Causeway.

The causeway affords the best view of **7** **Sarasota**★★ *(Visitor Center 941-957-1877)*, a bright, clean town with a modest skyline. Turn left on Tamiami Trail (US 41) and drive about 3 miles up to the **John and Mable Ringling Museum of Art**★★ *(5401 Bayshore Rd. 941-359-5700. Adm. fee)*, built in 1927, which Ringling gave to the state in 1936 after many years of wintering his circus in Sarasota. One of the Southeast's preeminent cultural institutions, the museum is an unbridled competition between jaw-dropping architecture and priceless paintings. The triumphal entrance immediately grabs your attention with its soaring arches and classical sculptures; you can almost hear Ringling off in the wings announcing, "And now, ladies and gentlemen, the greatest art on earth. . ." Architectural embellishments continue inside, where cavernous rooms three stories high display magnificent works by the likes of Rubens, van Dyck, and Tiepolo. The museum is just the beginning. Step out into the formal courtyard for sculpture and exquisite views of the bay. Then walk over to **Ca d'Zan**★★, Ringling's Venetian Renaissance-style palace. After a tour of the treasures inside, stand on the marble terrace for an aristocrat's-eye view of Sarasota Bay. Sunset burnishes the terra-cotta mansion a rich amber.

Push south on Tamiami to **Sarasota Jungle Gardens** *(3701 Bayshore Rd. 941-355-5305. Adm. fee)*. Opened in 1940, this old Florida-style attraction features paths winding through dense foliage, a flamingo lagoon, bird shows, and Biblical plants. If you prefer a purer, more adult-oriented horticultural experience, try **Marie Selby Botanical Gardens**★ *(Just S of causeway, 811 S. Palm Ave. 941-366-5731. Adm. fee)*. Displaying more than 20,000 tropical plants on 8.5 acres, the gardens are acclaimed for their orchids and epiphytes; a walkway through a bamboo grove ends at a meditative view of the bay.

For one more outdoor event, make a 14-mile excursion east on Fla. 72 to **Myakka River State Park**★ *(941-361-6511. Adm. fee)*, one of the state's oldest and largest parks. The tram and airboat tours are informative, fun, and popular; or you can rent a bike or a canoe and explore the native flora and fauna on your own. The park claims 7 miles of paved road, 12 miles of river, several hiking trails, and a lake—all in a primeval gathering of woods, prairie, and marsh.

It's an easy scoot from here up I-75 to Tampa.

23

Sarasota Jungle Gardens

Miami and the Keys★★

● 240 miles ● 3 days ● Year-round ● For lower rates
and fewer crowds travel off-season, June-Nov. Expect
heavy traffic on the Overseas Highway in season.

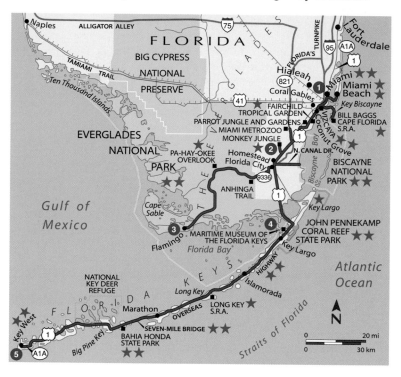

24

A drive of startling beauty, this road trip ranks among
the most scenic in the United States. From the upthrust
architecture of Miami to the horizontal sweep of the Everglades and the limpid aquamarine reefs of the Florida
Keys, the drive keeps you awestruck. Only one road goes
to the southernmost point in the continental United
States, so this is a one-way trip—appropriately enough,
for once in Key West many people choose never to leave.

Beginning in Miami with the art deco landscapes of
Miami Beach and the opulent Mediterranean showplaces
of Coral Gables, the drive moves persistently south. After
stopping at several commercial jungle gardens and Biscayne National Park, you strike southwest for an excursion
across the marshy bird-filled backwaters of Everglades
National Park. Then it's on to the keys for a 100-mile
odyssey down the Overseas Highway. You end in Key
West, that charming oddball of southern towns, where
every sunset is a cause for celebration.

Brash newcomer to Florida, ❶ **Miami**★★ *(Convention & Visitors Bureau, 701 Brickell Ave. 305-539-3000)* sprouted to life when Henry Flagler extended his Florida East Coast Railway down here in 1896, a year after a killer freeze ruined his orange crops in the northern part of the state.

Venetian Causeway and the Miami skyline

Travelers and businesses have been flocking to the Sunshine City ever since. A highlights tour starts in **Miami Beach**★★, a 10-mile strand weighted with behemoth hotels, many of them financed by the Mafia in the 1930s. In South Beach, visit the **Bass Museum of Art** *(2121 Park Ave. 305-673- 7530. Closed Mon.; adm. fee)*. The coral stone building is devoted to Renaissance religious art, paintings by Rubens, Bol, Jordaens, and temporary exhibits. Walk or drive a few blocks southwest to the **Holocaust Memorial**★★ *(1933-45 Meridian Ave. 305-538-1663)*, an eerily effective sculpture garden dedicated to the Jews who perished during World War II. Walk around the vine-draped circular plaza, with its granite walls laminated in photographs and inscribed with a chronological history of the genocide. A central bronze sculpture depicts a 42-foot-tall arm upon which emaciated figures desperately cling.

Miami Beach's Art Deco District

Like a transplanted New York, the Miami Beach area offsets dense blocks and grimy sidewalks with chummy neighborhood restaurants and bars. But as you continue down Collins Avenue and then Ocean Drive, it's a different story. Enjoying a spirited rebirth, the famous **Art Deco District**★★ features hundreds of jazzy buildings outfitted

Poling canoes through the Everglades

with neon, glass brick, and bright paint. Traffic crawls from 15th to 6th Street, so it's best to walk. Find yourself a seat at one of the many sidewalk hotel bars and enjoy the amazing procession of glamour day and night. If you don't spot an actual movie star or super model, you'll at least see people who ought to be.

Take the General MacArthur Causeway (US 41/Fla. A1A) across Biscayne Bay for a superlative view of Miami's bold skyline. The **Historical Museum of Southern Florida** *(Metro-Dade Cultural Center, 101 W. Flagler St. 305-375-1492. Adm. fee)* offers a brief overview of 10,000 years of Miami-area history. Included are exhibits on tourism, boom-time architecture, the Everglades, and Cuban immigrants.

Alligator, Everglades National Park

For a relatively secluded beach nearby, drive out to the end of **Key Biscayne** *(Toll)* and enter the **Bill Baggs Cape Florida State Recreation Area**★ *(305-361-5811. Adm. fee)*. Nature trails course the 415-acre park, and a 1.25-mile beach offers white sand and turquoise water for sunning and bathing.

Back on the mainland, head south on Bayshore Drive (Miami Avenue) a short distance to **Vizcaya**★★ *(3251 S. Miami Ave. 305-250-9133. Adm. fee)*, the regal Italian Renaissance-style villa built by industrialist James Deering in 1916. European decorative arts fill 34 rooms and splendid views overlook the formal gardens. Outside, a barge-

shaped stone breakwater accentuates the magnificent view of Biscayne Bay.

Staying south on Bayshore Drive brings you to the suburb of **Coconut Grove,** an early seaside settlement that manages to maintain its village identity. Lush with bougainvillea and banyans, the area has become an eclectic jumble of artist bungalows, swish boutiques, and hot nightclubs.

Driving south on Old Cutler Road takes you through a bayside neighborhood that includes **Fairchild Tropical Garden** ★ *(10901 Old Cutler Rd. 305-667-1651. Adm. fee).* The 83-acre botanical wonderland was tossed into a tropical salad by Hurricane Andrew in 1992, but it is green again with ferns, flowering shrubs, lily pools, and jungle backdrops. The **Parrot Jungle and Gardens** *(11000 S.W. 57th Ave. 305-666-7834. Adm. fee)* is a 1930s tourist mecca featuring paths through lush plantings and past talking birds, as well as tortoises, flamingos, and monkeys. A trained-bird show and petting zoo are just right for children.

The cageless **Miami Metrozoo** *(12400 S.W. 152nd St. 305-251-0400. Adm. fee)* has nearly 300 landscaped acres upon which animals from Africa, Asia, and Australia roam. You can ride a tram or monorail around the park, or walk a 3-mile trail. Just south, the low-key ❷ **Monkey Jungle** ★ *(3 miles W of US 1, 14805 S.W. 216th St. 305-235-1611. Adm. fee)* specializes in primates. Squirrel monkeys dig into the boxes of raisins that visitors are allowed to offer them; crab-eating macaques swim for food tossed into their pond; and spider monkeys and gibbons swing in their enclosures.

The main corridor south through here is US 1, a frankly dreary stretch of transmission shops, exotic dancing joints, and tract housing that pushes up against the Everglades. But by the time you're south of the Monkey Jungle, you've just about left development behind. Between Homestead and Florida City, travel east 9 miles on N. Canal Drive (S.W. 378th Street) to **Biscayne National Park** ★ ★ *(305-230-7275).* Land comprises only 5 percent of this aquatic paradise, a vast expanse of blue-green water shared by tropical fish, waterbirds, and other marine animals. A Visitor Center has videos and exhibits on the park's ecosystems, and a concessionaire offers glass-bottom boat tours and snorkel and scuba excursions.

Double Reefs

The 150-mile-long arc of coral reefs extending from Key Biscayne down to the Dry Tortugas runs in two distinct chains. Farthest from shore, the outer reefs are known for such big branch corals as staghorn and elkhorn. With water 10 to 60 feet deep, this zone supports sharks, barracudas, and other large fish. Patch reefs form in shallower water, buffered from waves by the outer reef layer. Here, more delicate corals such as sea fans and brain coral can grow, and a rainbow-spectrum of tropical fish flourish. Scuba divers take to the outer reefs; snorkelers prefer the gentler patch reefs.

27

Fish billboard, Key Largo

Roadside Bizarre

If Florida didn't invent weird and wacky roadside attractions, it certainly perfected the art. Alligator farms, wax museums, and floral exotica in the 1920s and '30s were the lure for getting you to stop at gift shops bloated with rubber snakes, plastic flamingos, and canned sunshine. A few of these early oddities still survive, like the **Cypress Knee Museum** (US 27. 941-675-2951) in Palmdale. Its hand-lettered roadside signs are an attraction in themselves ("Lady, If He Won't Stop, Hit Him on Head with Shoe"). Or the 60-year-old **Everglades Wonder Gardens** (27180 US 41. 941-992-2591) in Bonita Springs, which exhibits shark and horse embryos along with a bunch of caged animals.

28

Back on US 1, drive south and then west on Fla. 9336 through a patchwork sea of strawberry fields, sugarcane, and tropical nursery plants. After about 10 miles you arrive at the entrance to the 1.5-million-acre **Everglades National Park**★★ (305-242-7700. Adm. fee), whose mangrove swamps and saw-grass prairies the Native Americans called *pa-hay-okee*, or "grassy waters." Maps at the entrance station will get you underway, but it's a good idea to stop at the entrance Visitor Center for more visual information and help in planning your visit.

The main park road wanders 38 miles down to the tourist town of Flamingo. Several short nature trails along the way give you a good idea of the variety of Everglades scenery. The first and most popular stop, at the Royal Palm Visitor Center, offers two trails. The 0.5-mile **Anhinga Trail,** loops a slough frequented by alligators and plumed birds such as egrets and herons.

Starting in 1905, engineers began draining water from the Everglades for nearby population centers, leaving the local wildlife to fend for itself. Despite conservation efforts, animals have suffered. As Miami's population has soared, the number of wading birds has declined—93 percent since the 1930s.

A little farther along, the **Pa-hay-okee Overlook**★ has a boardwalk leading to an observation deck where you can view an enormous landscape of grasslands—accessible only to canoeists with skills to navigate the maze of narrow waterways around dense hammocks.

Down in ❸ **Flamingo,** the waters are more accessible and you can rent a canoe or take a cruise into the wetlands or bay. Once home to renegades and plume hunters, this busy terminus now offers a campground, a hotel, a Visitor Center, and a restaurant and bar with a view onto Florida Bay.

Retrace your steps back to US 1 and head south. Mangroves and lowlying foliage line the roadside as you cross the first of 42 bridges and begin to thread that necklace of coral jewels known as the Florida Keys. The longest one, 30-mile **Key Largo**★ (Chamber of Commerce 305-451-1414) introduces itself with marinas, bait-and-tackle shops, and some 25 dive operators—in a town of 15,000 souls. Mileposts on US 1 (descending as you travel south) are used for addresses. Drive down to Mile 102.5 and turn left for the **John Pennekamp Coral Reef State Park**★★ (305-451-1202. Adm. fee). The country's first

Florida

underwater park extends about 3 miles into the ocean
and 25 miles along the shore. Though the water is usually
clear enough to see for more than 100 feet, for best views
you need to get beneath the surface, where an extravagant undersea garden of color and motion rivets your
attention. More than 600 species of fish and 40 kinds of
coral inhabit these waters. A park concessionaire is fully
stocked with ways to get you under, from scuba instruc-
tion to snorkel tours and equipment rentals.

Across the highway, the ❹ **Maritime Museum of the
Florida Keys** *(305-451-6444. Closed Thurs.; adm. fee)* contains
rare treasures and artifacts recovered from sunken ships
dating from the 17th century. And a good local haunt for
seafood and key lime pie is **Jim & Val's Tugboat Restaurant** *(Off Mile 99, 2 Seagate Blvd. 305-453-9010)*. Down the
road, the **Florida Keys Wild Bird Rehabilitation Center**
(Mile 93.6. 305-852-4486. Donation) takes in a variety of
shore and forest birds, most injured by fishing lines.

South of Key Largo, the road is lined by hibiscus and
palms, with views of emerald waters opening up
on either side. In the early morning and other
lightly traveled times you almost feel as if you're
flying over the sea. This compelling road, the
Overseas Highway★★ was built along the bed
of Henry Flagler's 1912 railroad. An awesome feat
of construction in its time, the railroad was wiped
out by a hurricane in 1935.

Continue down to Long Key, stopping at **Long
Key State Recreation Area**★ *(Mile 67.5. 305-664-
4815. Adm. fee)* for a quiet commune with nature
along lagoon and beachside on the 1.25-mile
Golden Orb Trail. Soon you're driving across the
breathtaking **Seven Mile Bridge**★★, one of the
longest bridges in the world. To your right is an
older version of the bridge, now for pedestrians
only. The panorama of ocean and bay grows
more and more vividly green as you head southwest. Though the road is the thrilling attraction for
miles and miles, one more worthwhile turnout
just after the bridge takes you to **Bahia Honda
State Park**★★ *(Mile 36.8. 305-872-2353. Adm. fee)*. Claim-
ing one of the best beaches in the keys (where sandy
beaches are rare), this attractive park also has a mangrove
forest and hardwood hammock with such unusual West
Indian plants as the orange-flowering geiger tree, the yellow Alamanda, and the Jamaican morning glory. At a con-
cession stand here you can pick up a snack, rent a boat

John Pennekamp Coral Reef State Park

29

or snorkel equipment, or sign up for a parasail ride.

The next major island, **Big Pine Key,** is known for its diminutive Key deer, the smallest subspecies of the white-tailed deer on the continent. Though protected by the National Key Deer Refuge, the declining population numbers about 300. Since 1995, more than 200 have been killed by cars on the highway.

Continue to the end of the line—**Key West**★★ (*Chamber of Commerce 305-294-2587*), 150 miles from Miami and 90 from Havana, Cuba. One of the the state's largest and richest cities in the 1880s, it is now one of its

30

Florida Keys

most outlandish and endearing. To get downtown, follow signs for Fla. A1A (beaches/airport) to the left, not to the right (historic district). Both ways lead to the historic district, but the ocean drive is prettier with less traffic, and it takes you right past the **East Martello Museum & Gallery**★ (*3501 S. Roosevelt Blvd. 305-296-3913. Adm. fee*), a perfect place to start. Housed in a Civil War-era fort, this haphazard collection nonetheless gives a fine overview of the island's flavor, with exhibits on pirates, shipbuilders, rumrunners, and railroaders. A gallery of island eccentrics offers a glimpse at the characters that have washed up here—people like the Iguana Man, who used to bike around town with a half-dozen reptiles slung across his back and perched on the handlebars of his bike.

In the historic district, tour the house of another eccentric, the **Ernest Hemingway Home and Museum**★ (*907 Whitehead St. 305-294-1136. Adm. fee*). The legendary writer owned this large Spanish colonial-style home from 1931 to 1961 and penned most of his masterpieces in the backyard studio. In addition to his furniture and swimming pool, you'll see nearly 50 cats, descended from Hemingway's own.

For a panoramic view of the island and surrounding waters, climb the 90-foot **Key West Lighthouse Museum**★ (*938 Whitehead St. 305-294-0012. Adm. fee*). From up here you can also survey the distinctive Bahamian-inspired architecture—light and breezy verandas, raised foundations, and tin roofs.

Adrift off the keys

Not far away, the **Harry S Truman Little White House** ★ *(111 Front St. 305-294-9911. Adm. fee)*, favored retreat of the 33rd President, stands on the grounds of a former submarine base. Thirty-minute tours paint a portrait of Truman and his presidential successors Eisenhower and Kennedy on holiday here.

Nearby Duval Street, once low-key, now churns with noisy bars, T-shirt shops, and an endless parade of lock-stepped honeymooners and tattooed drifters, men in pirate bandanas and tourists on mopeds. What keeps this street from becoming just another generic hip locale are landmarks like the **Wrecker's Museum** *(322 Duval St. 305-294-9502. Adm. fee)*, a repository of Key West lore in what is considered the town's oldest house (1829). Rooms are furnished in period, and exhibits show how salvaging shipwrecks once made Key West the country's wealthiest town. Down at Greene and Front Streets, the **Mel Fisher Maritime Heritage Society** ★ *(305-294-2633. Adm. fee)* exhibits gold, silver, and other booty recovered from two Spanish galleons that sank 25 miles offshore in a 1622 hurricane. Fisher spent 16 years in search of the treasure, worth about 400 million dollars.

Now walk over to **Mallory Square** ★, the former shipwrecking hub that today draws tourists to its congeries of shell shops, tropical-drink bars, and tour vendors. Mallory is most famous for its nightly sunset-watching ritual. Jugglers, magicians, ropewalkers, and tarot-card readers entertain a dockside crowd, while the ocean and sky shimmer with soft colors . . . as another day at the end of the road draws to a close.

Ropewalker at Key West's daily sunset celebration

Northeast Coast★★

Taking off from the Orlando area and shooting up the coast, this trip interplays the speed and power of modern Florida with the natural beauty and graceful architecture of the long past. At least at first, it will keep you busy—walking, ogling, driving hard, and mapping out plans for beating the crowds. But the sights are definitely worth the effort. Then you can relax as you hit the beaches, and settle into a more leisurely rhythm.

The drive opens with the twin titans of Florida tourism, Orlando and the Kennedy Space Center—one a monument to artifice, the other to scientific achievement. Just up the way, Daytona Beach and its international speedway make the triangle of superpowers complete. After the multiple stimulations of megatheme parks and high-flying technology, superlatives begin to seem commonplace. It's time now for scenic Fla. A1A up along quiet shores and small communities to an uncommon place—Spanish-colonial St. Augustine, the oldest permanent European city in the country. Continuing to the northeast corner of the state, the route pauses at lovely barrier islands and nature preserves, before ending in Jacksonville.

Tripling its population in the past 25 years, ❶ **Orlando**★★ *(Information Center, 8445 International Dr. 407-363-5871)* is still one of the country's fastest growing cities. Among the world's top tourist destinations, it started its explosion in the early sixties when Walt Disney quietly bought up 30,000 acres of adjacent swampland and began converting it into an entertainment empire. As well as numerous ancillary water parks and resorts, the area today swaggers with five theme parks, a royal flush of play-worlds expertly packaged for mass appeal. Clear highway signs make getting around easy. But the crush of people in the parks can mar your visit. Some tips: Busiest times are weekends and school holidays. Arrive at the gate at least 30 minutes before opening time and go first to the most popular attractions. Tag small children with IDs.

The **Walt Disney World**★ *(Off I-4. 407-824-4321. Parking fee)* complex encompasses three separate parks. The original one, the **Magic Kingdom** *(Adm. fee)* has the iconic Cinderella Castle, surrounded by various lands and rides—Fantasyland, Adventureland, and Tomorrowland. Already looking worn-out, **Epcot** *(Adm. fee)* soldiers on with its gizmo-happy vision of the future and its country exhibitions. The newest extravagance, **Disney-MGM Studios**★ *(Adm. fee)* opened in 1989 and offers perhaps the most bang for the buck, with its rides and studio tours.

Disney-MGM Studios, Walt Disney World

Likewise, **Universal Studios** *(Off I-4. 407-363-8000. Adm. and parking fees)*, geared for older children and adults, invites you to "ride the movies" in its simulation chambers. Somewhat harder-edged than Disney-MGM, this park would get high marks if not for its intolerably long lines. And nearby **Sea World**★ *(Off I-4. 407-351-3600. Adm. and parking fees)* offers a good simulated helicopter ride, water-skiing shows, and trained animals.

Head east on the Bee Line Expressway *(toll)* about 40 miles to Fla. 407 north. At Fla. 405 go east a short distance to the **U.S. Astronaut Hall of Fame**★ *(6225 Vectorspace Blvd. 407-269-6100. Adm. fee)*, a good introduction to the space program. Videos and computer displays recount stories of each of the first 20 U.S. astronauts, re-creating the heroics and thrill of early space travel. Simulators offer a hint of space-flight training.

Take the causeway across the Indian River to Merritt Island and the ❷ **Kennedy Space Center Visitor Center**★★ *(Off Fla. 405. 407-452-2121. Arrive early and buy tickets for movies and tours right away)*, where you can immerse yourself in the legend and lore of NASA. Every satellite and manned rocket since the beginning of the space program in 1958 has lifted off from this bulge in

Florida's Atlantic seaboard. Two IMAX theaters screen wonderfully huge and realistic movies, including footage shot in space. Also very popular are the two-hour bus tours of the compound: The Kennedy Space Center Tour visits the shuttle launch areas and the new Apollo/Saturn V Center, while the Cape Canaveral Tour looks at the Mercury facilities and other historical sites on the cape. The Visitor Center holds a moon rock, real and mock-up spacecrafts, spacesuits, and other gear.

Engines of a Saturn 1B, Kennedy Space Center

NASA owns the interwoven 140,000-acre tract of forest, marsh, and shore defined as the **Merritt Island National Wildlife Refuge**★★ *(Off Rte. 402, E of Titusville. 407-861-0667. Closed for launches; call for schedule)*. A 7-mile wildlife drive courses along an impoundment dike and gets you close to shorebirds. Down at Playalinda Beach, part of **Canaveral National Seashore**★★ *(407-267-1110. Adm. fee)*, bask in a gloriously empty stretch of virgin coastline, favored by sea turtles and pelicans. Extending 25 miles north, the seashore preserves the longest undeveloped beach on Florida's east coast. From the dunes you can just see the towering assembly building and shuttle gantries on the south horizon—the most advanced technology in the world rising from the edge of wilderness.

Drive up I-95 and take the Port Orange exit for **Daytona Beach**★ *(Chamber of Commerce 904-255-0981)*, the birthplace of speed. But first, have a look at the area's past—**Sugar Mill Botanical Gardens** *(Old Sugar Mill Rd., 1 mile W of US 1, just N of Fla. 421. 904-767-1735)* contains the ruins of a sugar mill burned by Seminole in the 1830s. Shaded by live oaks, the 12-acre plot also holds several concrete dinosaurs left from a 1950s theme park.

For a view of the ocean and beach, cross the Halifax River and drive south about 5 miles on South Atlantic Avenue to the **Ponce de Leon Inlet Lighthouse**★ *(904-761-1821. Adm. fee)*. Take a look at the fine collection of nautical items in the 19th-century keepers' dwellings, then climb 203 steps to the top of the 175-foot-tall working light. If the climb doesn't take your breath away, the view will. The 23-mile strand of beach down below attracted automobile racers here as early as 1903. By 1935, they had pushed the land speed record up to 276 miles an hour; in the late fifties—to protect crowds and drivers—the sport was moved off the beach and onto a track.

Motorists may still drive on the wide, hard-packed beach. Follow Fla. A1A just north to the **Main Street Pier** and ramp down to the sand *(fee for beach parking and driving)*. From February to April, Atlantic Avenue (Fla. A1A) and the beach are a zoo of racing fans, motorcyclists, and college kids. The rest of the year stays fairly low-key and family style, with daytime action focusing on the **Boardwalk** *(Just N of pier, Main to Ora Sts. 904-238-1212)*, a promenade from the 1930s with eateries, video arcades, a sky lift, and other seaside amusements.

Just west, Daytona International Speedway's slick new attraction, ❸ **Daytona USA**★ *(1801 W. International Speedway Blvd. 904-947-6782. Adm. fee)* opened in July 1996. The fast-paced exhibit hall features Sir Malcolm Campbell's 1935 record-breaking Bluebird V, historic footage, interactive consoles, and live shows. A 70-mm movie version of the Daytona 500 offers a heart-pumping 14-minute distillation of race day, capturing the sport's furious speed. Speedway tours *(fee)* cover the pits and the 2.5-mile track with its 31-degree banks.

Motor back to the beach and head up Fla. A1A about 5 miles to Ormond Beach. A left on Granada Avenue takes you to John D. Rockefeller's restored winter home, **The Casements** *(25 Riverside Dr., SE of Ormond Bridge. 904-676-3216. Closed Sun.; donation)*. The oil magnate entertained racers and celebrities in this modest mansion from 1918 until his death in 1937; some of his furnishings are on display.

North on Fla. A1A, the roadside softens to beach houses and a few five-story condos—half the size of those in Daytona. The highway becomes two-lane, with some fine views of beaches framed by saw palmetto and Spanish bayonet. The **Gamble Rogers Memorial State Recreation Area at Flagler Beach** *(10.5 miles N of Ormond Beach. 904-517-2086. Adm. fee)* has acreage on the beach and

Daytona Beach

inland waterways for fishing, picnicking, and swimming.

Continue up the string of land that runs between the Atlantic and the Intracoastal Waterway. Small-town Flagler Beach has a fishing pier and a handful of little restaurants. Worth stopping for, even if you're just passing through: The 1920s **Topaz Hotel** *(Fla. A1A, just S of pier. 904-439-3275)*, an unassuming rendition of Mediterranean Revival, has a cozy Victorian parlor with a Victrola, player piano, human hair wreath, and antique toy collection. An adjoining restaurant *(dinner only, Tues.-Sat.)* offers a creative blend of elegance and down-home cooking. Guests stay in original rooms or in the newer, flanking motel.

About 13 miles north, turn left for **Washington Oaks State Gardens** *(904-446-6780. Adm. fee)*. This 400-acre chunk of beach and coastal hammock was once part of a plantation owned by a general in the Second Seminole War. Formal gardens and reflecting pools lie by the languid Matanzas River. You can swim at the beach across the highway, but watch out for coquina boulders with sharp edges.

Just north, cross Matanzas Inlet, where fishermen cast in the surf and birds wheel above the breakers. This lovely scene was the setting for mass horror in 1565 when Pedro Menéndez and his Spanish soldiers confronted a hostile contingent of French Huguenots. Wrecked by a hurricane, the French landed south of the inlet. Menéndez convinced them to surrender, brought them across in boats, fed them, then took them behind the dunes and bayoneted them. Amazingly, he pulled the same trick on an even larger group of Frenchmen 12 days later, for a total kill of nearly 250. Menéndez's base of operations developed into St. Augustine, the country's oldest permanent European city. Before driving up, have a look at ❹ **Fort Matanzas National Monument** *(8635 Fla. A1A. 904-471-0116)*. To fend off the British, the Spanish built the small coquina fortress in 1742; a free ferry takes visitors out to the fort, islanded in the Matanzas River.

Up ahead, climb the **St. Augustine Lighthouse**★ *(81 Lighthouse Ave. 904-829-0745. Adm. fee)* for bracing views of sea and land all around. An adjacent museum outlines the work of lightkeepers, who lived here from 1874 to 1955.

Castillo de San Marcos National Monument

Now cross the Bridge of Lions into downtown St. **Augustine**★★*(Visitor Center 904-825-1000)*. The bridge offers picturesque views of the old city's coquina walls and red-tiled roofs, its moored sailboats and crenellated battlements. Turn right for the Visitor Center and **Castillo de San Marcos National Monument**★★ *(1 Castillo Dr. 904-829-6506. Adm. fee)*, another place for noteworthy vistas. Its gray

Spanish Quarter Museum, St. Augustine

walls now encrusted with algae, the fort was started in 1672. Listen to a ranger program, then ramble through the barrel-vaulted chambers and atop the gundeck, trying to get a handle on 300 years of history. You'll hear the words "old and oldest" used a lot in this town, but the Castillo is the real thing—the oldest structure in town and the oldest masonry fort in the country.

Stroll down St. George Street, the north end lined with gift shops and cafés, as well as intriguing alleys that lead off to houses tucked behind shady gardens. The **Spanish Quarter Museum**★ *(33 St. George St. 904-825-6830. Adm. fee)* is a living history complex of restored and reconstructed houses that illustrate 18th-century colonial Spanish lifestyles.

Below the Plaza de la Constitución, the **Ximenez-Fatio House**★ *(20 Aviles St. 904-829-3575. Thurs.-Sun., closed Sept.)*, dating from around 1798, is appointed to reflect its days as an 1830s boardinghouse, each room set up with a different theme, including nautical, artistic, and familial motifs. And a few blocks southeast, the **Oldest House**★ *(14 St. Francis St. 904-824-2872. Adm. fee)*—also called the González-Alvarez House—was built in the early 1700s and is furnished to show its Spanish, English, and American occupations. Museum rooms and a courtyard round out this fascinating site.

For an example of the indelible stamp railroad tycoon Henry Flagler left on the area, walk over to the **Lightner Museum**★ *(King and Cordova Sts. 904-824-2874. Adm. fee)*. The opulence of Flagler's twin-towered Hotel Alcazar (1888) makes a fitting receptacle for this staggering three-floor collection of Chinese antiquities, Tiffany lamps, and other treasures. Then cross the street to the even more grandiose **Flagler College** (the former Hotel Ponce de Leon), a Spanish Renaissance castle of towers, arches, and terra-cotta, mosaic-tile floors, and a gilded dome.

Continue north on Fla. A1A, through a scenic stretch of wild dunes flashing ocean views. A few miles south of Ponte Vedra Beach you begin to hit seaside development, which thickens into suburbia by Atlantic Beach. But as you head

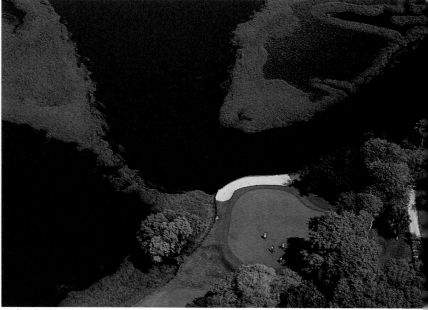

Amelia Island

up toward Mayport, you magically find yourself back in the clear again. Occupying a point of land at the mouth of St. Johns River, the Mayport Naval Station ranks as one of the nation's largest naval bases, harboring helicopters, frigates, destroyers, and guided-missile cruisers. From the rustic fishing village of Mayport, catch the **St. Johns River Ferry** *(904-270-2520. Every 30 min.; fare)* across to Fort George Island.

A half mile north of the ferry landing, turn left for **Kingsley Plantation**★ *(3 miles W of Fla. A1A. 904-251-3537)*, lying at the end of a sandy road that tunnels under pines and cabbage palms. Situated at the southern extreme of the Sea Island chain, this plantation merits a visit for its rapturous riverside setting and its compelling exhibits on slave life and slave trading—made more interesting when you realize that the master had initially purchased his wife

as a slave. From 1814 to 1839, the Kingsleys grew cotton, citrus, cane, and corn here; the main house, kitchen, tabby barn, and slave house ruins remain.

Take Fla. A1A north across the Fort George River to **Little Talbot Island State Park**★★ *(904-251-2320. Adm. fee)*, a vision of what a beach park should be. Boardwalks lead over an extensive range of dunes and sea oats to a wide, secluded seashore 5 miles long. A 4-mile nature trail cuts through a lush coastal hammock and around to the beach. The park owns part of the next island, Big Talbot, as well as the southern tip of Amelia Island. The route up is one of the state's prettiest: Drive past the bluffs of Big Talbot and across Nassau Sound to **Amelia Island**★, a barrier island banked with sun-sanctified marshes and immaculate sands. The last few miles slow down somewhat as you thread a long row of beach cottages. As you approach the tip of the island, make a left and a quick right for **Fort Clinch State Park**★ *(2601 Atlantic Ave. 904-277-7274. Adm. fee)*. Then drive 3 miles through a canopy of moss-hung oaks that print a paisley pattern of sunlight on the road. The well-preserved fort *(fee)* was captured by Federals early in the Civil War without any bloodshed. Walk on the ramparts for superior views of the inlet and ocean—across the wide sound lies pristine Cumberland Island, Georgia.

Drive on into the town of **Fernandina Beach** and through the charming 6-block downtown. Among the shops and restaurants, the 1878 **Palace Saloon** *(Centre St. and 2nd Ave. 904-261-6320)* is an eye-catcher with its maritime murals, pressed-tin ceiling, and 40-foot mahogany bar.

Now go south to ❺ **Jacksonville** *(Chamber of Commerce 904-366-6600)*, a brawny port city, pumping with commerce and industry on the St. Johns River. On the way in, stop off for a tour of **Anheuser-Busch Brewery** *(111 Busch Dr. 904-751-8116)* and a free sample of their product. To the southeast of downtown, the **Jacksonville Museum of Contemporary Art** *(4160 Boulevard Center Dr. 904-398-8336. Closed Mon.; adm. fee)* showcases the very oldest and the very newest. The museum has an important collection of pre-Columbian artifacts and displays the work of local and state artists.

On the river's north side, the **Cummer Museum of Art and Gardens**★★ *(829 Riverside Ave. 904-356-6857. Closed Mon.; adm. fee)* presents a small but strong survey that progresses from ancient Roman artifacts to Renaissance and baroque paintings to works of Impressionism and modern art. Finish the drive with a stroll through the gardens out back for refreshing river views.

Two Henrys

After the Civil War and an 1873 depression, southern railroads were nearly out of steam. Loaded with ready money, two gentlemen from New England swooped in, snapped up foreclosed railways, and began extending their lines. Both originally came to Florida for the health of their wives—Henry Plant in 1861 and Henry Flagler in 1877. After establishing their territories—Plant on the west coast and Flagler on the east—they began a competitive working relationship, sitting on each other's boards and mapping out the development of Florida. Their first two major resort palaces were completed three years apart—Flagler's Ponce de Leon (St. Augustine) in 1888 and Plant's Tampa Bay Hotel in 1891. When Plant died in 1899 at age 80, Flagler was a pallbearer. Flagler himself died in 1913 at 83.

Mobile Bay Loop ★

● **175 miles** ● **2 days** ● **Year-round** ● **Mobile is most beautiful during the azalea bloom, from mid-March to mid-April. The Azalea Trail Festival (334-434-7304) takes place the last weekend in March.**

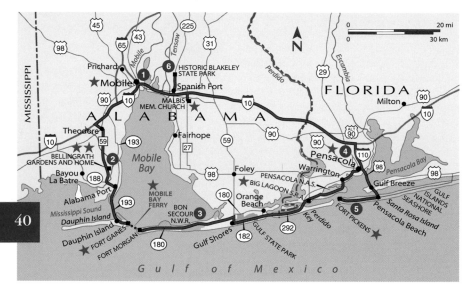

From Mobile to Pensacola and back, this short course in Gulf Coast history covers graceful old houses, Civil War forts, and the splendid scenery of Mobile Bay and the Gulf of Mexico. Mobile's historic districts and antebellum manses set the tone for your exploration into the colonial and Civil War heritage of the area. After driving south to renowned Bellingrath Gardens, the drive makes a short hop down to Dauphin Island and Fort Gaines. Next, you'll travel by ferry across the mouth of Mobile Bay, then continue along the seashore into Florida and up to Pensacola, another port city with a colorful pedigree and a world-class naval air museum. The interstate back to Mobile offers two surprises—a jewel of a Greek Orthodox church and one of the Civil War's last battlefields.

Before there was New Orleans, there was ❶ **Mobile★,** the French colonial capital until 1718. The city held on and grew into a trading and military center. Today Mobile is a city on the upswing, steadily recovering from the closing of a local air force base in the 1960s. Downtown, new buildings are rising, accented by a modernistic glass convention center and pedestrian bridge that gives great views of the busy port and its big tankers. Start at **Fort Condé** *(150 S. Royal St. 334-434-7304),* which doubles as the city's Welcome Center. A partial reconstruction of the early 18th-century fort holds excavated artifacts and dioramas on the fort under French, English, and Spanish rule.

A few blocks west, you can spend hours at the **Museum of Mobile**★ *(355 Government St. 334-434-7569. Closed Mon.)*, occupying an 1872 Italianate town house. Treasures include letters of Napoleon and George Washington, Union adm. David Farragut's chair, and a popular display of flashy Mardi Gras costumes.

At Dauphin and Claiborne Streets, gaze up at the twin belfries of the 1850 **Cathedral of the Immaculate Conception**★ *(334-434-1565);* inside, votive candles gutter and footsteps echo in the vaulted nave.

Three historic houses, all a short drive away, merit a visit. The **Richards-D.A.R. House**★ *(256 N. Joachim St. 334-434-7320. Closed Mon.; adm. fee)* makes an immediate statement with its showy ironwork of arabesques and scrolls, the city's fanciest. Having built **Oakleigh** *(350 Oakleigh Pl. 334-432-1281. Closed Sun.; adm. fee)* in the 1830s, cotton broker James Roper promptly went bankrupt, later died a pauper, and was buried in Church Street Cemetery. His house is now furnished to reflect upper-class life in late 19th-century Mobile. The city's largest house museum, the **Bragg-Mitchell Mansion** *(1906 Springhill Ave. 334-471-6364. Closed Sat.; adm. fee)* weighs in

41

Fort Condé, in Mobile

with massive mirrors, Chippendale chairs, and 15-foot ceilings. The Greek Revival home dates from 1855.

The **Battleship U.S.S.** *Alabama* ★ *(Off I-10, 2703 Battleship Pkwy. 334-433-2703. Adm. fee)* shot down 22 Japanese planes and destroyed enemy fortifications in World War II. You can tour the ship and an adjacent submarine.

Now head southwest out of town on I-10, and exit on County Rd. 59. After about 2 miles, follow signs to the left for ❷ **Bellingrath Gardens and Home**★★ *(334-973-2217 or 800-247-8420. Adm. fee)*. Alabama's horticultural tour de force began in 1918, when Coca-Cola bottler Walter Bellingrath bought a fishing camp on the Fowl River. He and his wife turned the property into a work of art and opened it to the public in 1932. You can walk the 65 landscaped acres in any season and behold a profusion of blooms. Especially appealing is the view from the brick patio, where a terraced lawn glides to the sequined river. The overstuffed house contains the Bellingrath's travel souvenirs, and crystal, furniture, and porcelain by Baccarat, Waterford, Belter, Mallard, Meissen, and Dresden.

Continue south to Ala. 188 east, then join Ala. 193 south across a series of causeways over the marshes. As you rise to the top of a bridge, you'll have breathtaking views of Mississippi Sound on the right and Mobile Bay on the left. Continue onto **Dauphin Island,** a generally low-key strand known for its pier and deep-sea fishing. On the island's eastern tip, **Fort Gaines** ★ *(334-861-6992. Adm. fee)* saw heavy action in the 1864 Battle of Mobile Bay. Despite a hellish barrage from Forts Gaines and Morgan, Admiral Farragut's intrepid fleet broke through to the bay and captured the forts, choking off Mobile's blockade runners. You can walk through and on top of the massive pentagonal fort. From the gun emplacements there are wonderful views of the bay, dotted by tremendous natural gas platforms.

Drive back to the marina and line up for the **Mobile Bay Ferry** ★ *(334-540-7787. Every 90 min.; fare)*. On the scenic 45-minute crossing, try to spot the lowlying Fort Gaines before it melts into the shoreline. Once on the other side, take a tour of Gaines's counterpart, **Fort Morgan** *(334-540-7125. Adm. fee)*.

A-4 Skyhawks at National Museum of Naval Aviation, Pensacola

East on Ala. 180 takes you past a few cottages on stilts and lots of low dunes blanketed with scrubby growth. In about 12 miles, watch for ❸ **Bon Secour National Wildlife Refuge** *(334-540-7720)*. The 6,500-acre preserve ranges from pine and oak woodlands to beach dunes. You can take a 2-mile nature trail out to the white-sand beach or drive the unmarked dirt road.

Minor development begins several miles west of the small town of Gulf Shores, followed by a good stretch of pristine seashore protected by **Gulf State Park** *(Ala. 182. 334-948-7275. Adm. fee)*. Continue east, cross a bridge onto Perdido Key, and in a few miles you're in Florida. Continue on Fla. 292 inland and follow signs for **Big Lagoon**

At the Lavalle House, Historic Pensacola Village

State Recreation Area ★ *(Cty. Rds. 293 and 292A. 904-492-1595. Adm. fee)*, a wonderful 700-acre spread along a salt marsh and tidal lagoon. The park road winds 2.5 miles to a picnic area, where a short trail leads to an observation tower that gives fine views of Perdido Key, the lagoon and Gulf, and herons wading in medallions of liquid sunlight.

Continue east on County Rd. 292A and south on Blue Angel Parkway (Fla. 173) to the back entrance of the Pensacola U.S. Naval Air Station. Signs direct you to the **National Museum of Naval Aviation** ★ ★ *(904-452-3604)*, a tremendous facility harboring more than 130 aircraft, including a formation of A-4 Skyhawks (Blue Angels) hanging in a seven-story glass atrium. Among the many virtual experiences here are a full-motion flight simulator and a seven-story, 15,000-watt IMAX theater.

Then drive up Radford and Taylor Roads to **Fort Barrancas** *(904-455-5167. Closed Mon.-Tues. Nov.-Feb.)*, one of four fortifications built in the early 19th century to secure Pensacola Bay. The Spanish built a fort on this bluff (barranca) in 1698; during the Civil War, Confederates used Barrancas to bomb Fort Pickens, across the water, but failed to dislodge the Federals.

Proceed east on Fla. 292 into ❹ **Pensacola** ★ *(Convention & Visitors Information Center, 1401 E. Gregory St. 904-434-1234 or 800-874-1234)*. If Don Tristan de Luna's settlement here in 1559 had taken hold, it would have become the country's oldest continuously settled European city, beating out St. Augustine by six years. Though that first attempt lasted only two years, the well-protected harbor was destined to become a port. Permanently settled in 1698, Pensacola ranks as Florida's second oldest city.

A grid of streets laid out by the British and renamed by

Mobile's Mardi Gras

If you want to do Mardi Gras without being drowned in a sea of humanity, try the country's original. Mobile can trace its pre-Lenten celebration back to 1703, besting the New Orleans festivities by more than a hundred years. An early band of revelers, stirring up the streets with cowbells and rakes, called themselves the Cowbellion de Rakin Society, thus initiating the esoteric world of Mardi Gras krewes and royalty. Two weeks of costume balls and parades culminate on Shrove Tuesday with elaborate floats and marching bands, free-flung beads and fake doubloons. A family-oriented, mostly local affair, Mobile's Mardi Gras does not go in for the bare bodies and drunken excesses of its neighbor city, but on the final day you can expect a crowd of at least 200,000. This is, after all, the state's biggest party.

43

the Spanish, the **Seville Historic District**★ *(Between Florida Blanca, Tarragona, Garden, and Main Sts.)* has numerous restored houses, ranging in style from Creole to frame vernacular to Victorian. For a good primer on city history, start with the **Pensacola Historical Museum** *(115 E. Zaragoza St. 904-433-1559. Closed Sun.; adm. fee),* housed in the 1882 Arbona Building. Within this district, **Historic Pensacola Village**★ *(Tickets at 205 E. Zaragoza St. 904-444-8905. Closed Sun. Labor Day–Mem. Day; adm. fee)* encompasses several houses and museums.

Yield to the siren call of the beaches and make a brief excursion south of the city. Take the bridge over beautiful Pensacola Bay to Pensacola Beach, then west 9 miles out to the **5 Fort Pickens**★ *(Adm. fee),* part of the **Gulf Islands National Seashore** *(904-934-2600).* The massive bastion, completed in 1834, served as a fortification and training ground for more than a century. Rangers offer fine tours, or you can scramble around on the thick walls yourself, enjoying views of the coast and Gulf.

Gulf Islands National Seashore

To get back to Mobile, breeze west on I-10 through an undeveloped land of tall pines and hardwoods. Along the way, head south on Ala. 181 and County Rd. 27. In less than a mile, you'll see a sight unusual in a countryside where even filling stations are rare. Three striking domes crown the towers of the **Malbis Memorial Church**★ *(334-626-3050),* a Byzantine-style Greek Orthodox church opened in 1964 by a community of Greek immigrants. Inside, rich mosaics and icons swirl below a blue vault of gold stars on a 75-foot-high central dome.

Go west one more exit on I-10 and take Ala. 225 north to **6 Historic Blakeley State Park** *(334-626-0798. Adm. fee),* 3,800 acres spread along the Tensaw River. This is where one of the last land encounters of the Civil War was fought. Dirt roads interlace the park and take you to an 18th-century French townsite and the breastworks and rifle pits left from the fighting that occurred here between never-say-die Confederate and Federal troops on April 9, 1865. By then, Lee had surrendered to Grant at Appomattox.

Black Belt Tour ★

● **440 miles** ● **3 to 4 days** ● **Year-round**

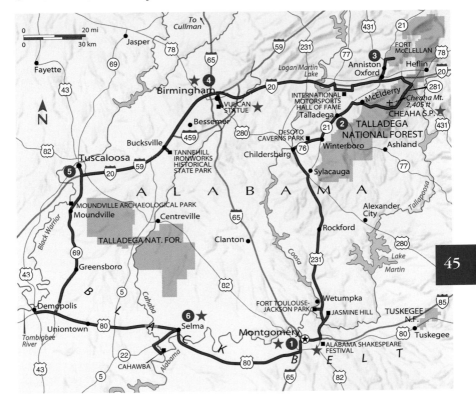

Circling the heartland of Alabama, this ambitious drive offers a cross section of the state's topography. The southern half of the loop roughly fits within the Black Belt, a broad band of dark, rich soil underlain by limestone, while the northern part explores the wooded hills surrounding Birmingham. In Montgomery, an easygoing state capital, you'll see how important events in Civil War and civil rights history collide in one place. Next travel north, into an area boasting some of the finest white marble in the world, then on to a national forest that reaches the state's highest point. After coasting down a scenic highway into Anniston, an Army post town loaded with fine museums, the drive enters Birmingham, whose industrial beginnings and civil rights struggles have earned it a lineup of star attractions. After a stop in Tuscaloosa at the august University of Alabama, you continue on into the historic cotton planting region and lovely Selma before returning to Montgomery.

Cotton wagon,
Old Alabama Town, Montgomery

A major cotton market in the 1800s, **❶ Montgomery**★ *(Visitor Center, 401 Madison Ave. 334-262-0013)* was the first—albeit brief—capital of the Confederacy. Overriding Jefferson Davis's veto, the Confederate Congress moved the capital to Richmond after four months. But while here, Davis ordered the bombing of Fort Sumter, starting the Civil War. Some say the war didn't end until nearly a century later, when the civil rights movement got underway here.

Civil Rights Memorial, Montgomery

Downtown Montgomery has an almost small-town feel. There's not much traffic and few high buildings, and it's easy to negotiate the orderly grid of streets. Start with a stroll through the 19th century in **Old Alabama Town** *(301 Columbus St. 334-240-4500 or 888-240-1850. Adm. fee).* A folksy audiotape tour guides you through this "town" of relocated buildings, including a one-room schoolhouse, country doctor's office, and shotgun-style house.

A few blocks southeast, the 1851 **Alabama State Capitol**★ *(Dexter Ave. and S. Bainbridge St. 334-242-3935. Closed Sun. Nov.-March)* is awash with history. A bronze star marks the approximate spot where Davis was sworn in as President of the Confederacy and where governors still take the oath of office—holding Davis's Bible. The 1965 Selma-to-Montgomery march for black voting rights ended at these steps. Inside, the spectacular twin two-story spiral staircases are attributed to the craftsmanship of a former slave.

Walk two blocks west to the **Civil Rights Memorial**★ *(400 Washington Ave.)*, a simple yet moving tribute to those who died in the struggle for equality. Water bubbles up from a black marble disc and flows evenly across the inscribed names. A guard stands duty here around the clock to protect the memorial from vandalism.

A block down the hill stands the unassuming **Dexter**

Avenue King Memorial Baptist Church *(454 Dexter Ave. 334-263-3970. Mon.-Sat., call for tour times and reservations; donation),* where Martin Luther King, Jr., was pastor from 1954 to 1960. An earlier pastor had suggested a bus boycott, but it took King's magnetism to put the civil rights protest (1955-56) into action. You can see the pulpit where he preached, then stand outside and look over to the capitol and imagine Davis's 1861 inaugural ceremonies there. Few places in the South give you such a sense of the great march of history.

East of town, the **Alabama Shakespeare Festival**★ *(1 Festival Dr. 334-271-5353 or 800-841-4273. Adm. fee for performances)* deserves special mention as one of the South's finest cultural centers. An unprecedented 21.5-million-dollar donation from Wynton Blount resulted in two theaters that stage nearly year-round productions of classical and contemporary works. The rolling grounds and serene lakes suggest England more than Alabama. Sharing the same verdant park, the **Montgomery Museum of Fine Arts** *(334-244-5700. Closed Mon.)* highlights such American painters as Whistler, Sargent, and Hopper, as well as displays works by F. Scott Fitzgerald's wife, Zelda, who grew up in Montgomery.

For a quick turn through ancient Greece, visit **Jasmine Hill** *(3001 Jasmine Hill Rd. 334-567-6463. Closed Mon.; adm. fee).* Starting in the 1930s, Benjamin and May Fitzpatrick transformed their 17-acre hilltop into a delightful garden to showcase their collection of reproductions of classical sculpture amassed during some 20 trips to Greece.

Travel north on US 231 to Wetumpka and follow signs 3 miles west on West Fort Toulouse Road to **Fort Toulouse-Jackson Park** *(334-567-3002. Adm. fee),* at the junction of the Coosa and Tallapoosa Rivers. In 1814, after he had devastated the Creek at nearby Horseshoe Bend, Andrew Jackson built this fort on the site of an old French military outpost. Here he signed the Treaty of Fort Jackson, taking 20 million acres from the Creek. You can walk inside the re-created French stockade and stroll by the river where Fort Jackson is being reconstructed.

Dexter Avenue King Memorial Baptist Church

Continue north through an unspectacular landscape of kudzu-coated hillocks, dotted with trailer houses. Gradually the terrain opens to broader views of the high hills to come. Not many small-town museums wear marble facades, but in **Sylacauga** *(Chamber of Commerce, 17 W. Fort Williams St. 205-249-0308)* marble is as common as grits.

47

The town sits atop a seam of pure white marble—32 miles long, 1.5 miles wide, and 400 feet deep. Quarried since the 1840s, the stone has been used in the Lincoln Memorial and other prominent buildings. The **Comer Museum**★ *(711 N. Broadway Ave. 205-245-4016. Tues.-Fri. or by appt.)* outlines local marble history and displays works by Italian sculptor Giuseppe Moretti, who operated a quarry here in the early 1900s. Memorabilia of native son Jim Nabors fill another large room.

Follow US 231 north to Ala. 76, then detour east 5 miles through peaceful farmlands to **DeSoto Caverns Park** *(205-378-7252. Adm. fee).* Legendary womb of the Creek Nation, the cave was used for burials more than 2,000 years ago. One-hour tours visit a Confederate gunpowder mining area; a Prohibition-era speakeasy; and the Great Cathedral room, featuring a sound-and-laser show.

Just north, the town of ❷ **Talladega** *(Chamber of Commerce, 210 East St. 205- 362-9075)* was where Andrew Jackson scored his first victory over the Creek in November 1813. Anchored by the columned courthouse, the square has a pleasantly predictable feel, with one flamboyant exception—the 1936 **Ritz Theatre,** a jazzy art deco cinema undergoing restoration. Drive east on South Street through the **Silk Stocking District,** boasting an unusually fine congregation of turn-of-the-century houses, graced by pillars, balconies, and porches.

In the Silk Stocking District, Talladega

About 6 miles northeast of Talladega on Ala. 21, watch for County Rd. 398. Take a right and swing into a section of the **Talladega National Forest** that covers the highest ground in the state. Look for another right turn at McElderry onto County Rd. 385. The road narrows now and begins a swishing climb through wooded hills. At one clear-cut area, you have good views of the distant rocky cliffs of **Cheaha State Park**★ *(Ala. 281. 205-488-5111. Adm. fee).* Once in the park, take the 2.5-mile loop road around Cheaha Mountain (Indian for "high"). The 30-foot observation tower stands some 2,400 feet above sea level—not terrifically high, but the panorama of folded hills and broad valleys gives you a lofty feeling. The 1-mile **Bald Rock Trail** brings you to gorgeous views of the rumpled val-ley far below. Breezes roll up these hills and sigh like ocean waves through the scrub pines. It's easy to find yourself wishing for wings.

Cheaha State Park

Leaving Cheaha, you travel north on part of the Talladega Scenic Byway (Ala. 281), one of the loveliest roads in the state. Curve down the mountain, fol-lowing signs northwest to Annis-ton; overlooks offer invigorating views. Planned as an iron com-pany and textile mill town in the 1870s, ❸ **Anniston** *(Chamber of Commerce, 1330 Quintard Ave. 205-237-3536 or 800-489-1087)* now turns out soldiers at Fort McClellan's training center. You go through several trafficky miles to get into town, but a number of attractions make it worth your time.

Go west on 18th Street about a mile to the **Church of St. Michael and All Angels** *(18th St. W. and Cobb Ave. 205-237-4011)*, a beacon of hope in a forlorn neighborhood. When the ironworks closed in the 1950s, this middle-class area began to deteriorate, but the 1890 Norman-style church remains well cared for. Walk around the stone building and through cloisters, then enter the dark sanctu-ary and see how many angels you can spot—carved in stone and wood, placed in niches, peering from beams.

North on Ala. 21 a couple of miles, turn right for the **Anniston Museum of Natural History**★ *(800 Museum Dr. 205-237-6766. Closed Mon.; adm. fee)*. What makes this well-conceived museum distinctive is its extensive collection of mounted animals donated by local big-game hunters. Next door, the new **Berman Museum**★ *(840 Museum Dr. 205-237-6261. Adm. fee)* presents weapons and armaments gathered from around the world by passionate collectors Farley and Germaine Berman. Some exquisitely crafted pieces include a Persian scimitar encrusted with nearly 1,300 rose-cut diamonds, Jefferson Davis's ivory-handled pistols, and Egyptian King Farouk's gold-and-jewel dagger.

Just north on Ala. 21, turn into Fort McClellan at the Summerall Gate and follow signs to the **Military Police Corps Regimental Museum** *(205-848-3522. Mon.-Fri. or by appt.)*, which outlines the history of MPs from the Revolu-tionary War to the present. Included are escape tools from a Vietnam POW camp, confiscated zip guns, and a piece of the rope used to hang Japanese war criminal General Tojo.

Return to Anniston and go west on I-20, exiting for the **International Motorsports Hall of Fame** *(Speedway Blvd. 205-362-5002. Adm. fee)*, where over a hundred cars fill a circular complex of buildings. See stock cars, dragsters, and the Budweiser rocket car—a 39-foot missile that accelerates to 400 miles an hour in 3 seconds. Then take a moment to reflect on what a 200-miles-an-hour racing speed can do to an automobile, as you view two cars totalled here at the Talladega Superspeedway.

Head west on the four-lane Speedway Boulevard (the next exit will get you back up to I-20). Cross Logan Martin Lake and continue west across a flat landscape that begins to step into hills by the time you reach ❹ **Birmingham** ★ *(Visitor Centers, 22nd St. N. and 9th Ave. N., and 12th St. and University Blvd. 205-458-8000 or 800-458-8085)*, the state's largest city.

The steel-manufacturing center of the 1870s has survived industrial blight and racial conflict to emerge as a likeable city of skyscrapers and parks. Start downtown at the highly impressive **Birmingham Museum of Art** ★ *(2000 8th Ave. N. 205-254-2566. Closed Mon.)* and take in a worldwide collection ranging from Ming dynasty Buddhas to paintings from the Italian Renaissance to 20th-century art. A two-story bay window gives onto a sculpture garden with works by Rodin and Botero.

At the International Motorsports Hall of Fame, near Talladega

A few blocks southwest, the **Birmingham Civil Rights Institute** ★ *(520 16th St. N. 205- 328-9696. Closed Mon.; adm. fee)* offers a dramatic walk through Birmingham's history. View a segregated streetcar, eavesdrop on racial talk in the 1950s, and experience other realistic settings of a divided city. The museum displays the door from the jail cell where Martin Luther King, Jr., wrote "Letter from a Birmingham Jail," and a window gives you a framed picture of the **Sixteenth Street Baptist Church** *(1530 6th Ave. N. 205-251-9402. Closed Mon.)*, where a 1963 bomb killed four girls. Across the street in **Kelly Ingram Park**, a center for demonstrations in the '60s, sculptures depict snarling police dogs and firehoses trained on protesters.

Visit the city's early history at **Sloss Furnaces** *(20 32nd St. N. 205-324-1911. Closed Mon.)*, a national historic landmark preserving the blast furnaces that churned out pig

Birmingham by night

iron for nearly 90 years. Considered an eyesore by some, the industrial complex was nearly razed, but preservationists recognized it as an important part of the city's heritage. Self-guided tours explain the complex iron-making process and the lives of the men who worked here.

A mile or so down First Avenue, **Five Points South** is a neighborhood full of shops and restaurants frequented by university students and professionals. The Spanish Revival architecture dates back more than a century, when the area was a separate town. The nearby **Vulcan Statue** ★ (*20th St. S. and Valley Ave. 205.328-2863. Adm. fee*), symbolizing the city's ironworking history, stands 56 feet tall atop a 125-foot observation tower that gives you the best view of the city and countryside.

The **Red Mountain Museum** (*2230 22nd St. S. 205-933-4153. Adm. fee*) takes advantage of a road cut to demonstrate 150 million years of geologic history. An interpretive path leads along the sheer rock wall; the museum has a good collection of fossils.

On I-20/59 southwest to Tuscaloosa, stop off at the **Tannehill Ironworks Historical State Park** (*Near Bucksville, 2 miles E of I-20/59. Follow signs. 205-477-5711. Adm. fee*) for a more in-depth look at the area's iron industry. The park preserves the ironworks that operated here between 1829 and 1865 and also features some 30 pioneer homes and buildings.

Continue on to ⑤ **Tuscaloosa** and pick up information at the **Jemison-Van de Graaff Mansion** (*1305 Greensboro Ave. 205-391-9200 or 800-538-8696*), the city's brand-new Visitor Center. Built in 1859 the Italianate creation ranks as the town's finest house with its conservatory and 18-foot ceilings. Alabama's capital from 1825 to 1847, Tuscaloosa is known today for the **University of Alabama.** This school is mighty proud of its football team, particularly under the tutelage of the most successful coach in the history of major college football. The **Paul W. Bryant Museum**★ *(300 Bryant Dr. 205-348-4668. Adm. fee)* offers 105 years of Crimson Tide football history, including the legendary Bryant years (1958-1982). A re-creation of his office and a crystal replica of his trademark houndstooth hat honor the coach. A few blocks west on campus, the **Alabama Museum of Natural History** *(205-348-7550. Adm. fee)* is a cornucopia of fossils, rocks, minerals, and animal heads. (Since the parking lot has no specific visitor spaces, unofficial policy is to ignore the ticket you'll likely get.)

Drive south on Ala. 69 through rolling forest and farmland and pull over for **Moundville Archaeological Park** *(205-371-2572. Adm. fee)*, where 26 flat-topped mounds were built between A.D. 900 and 1500 along what is now the Black Warrior River. The museum houses a good collection of pottery, tools, and other artifacts, including an elaborately inscribed cup and stone disc.

As you slice through the pastureland to the south, the red hills and hardwood forests begin to fall away, and views open up to rich plains where cotton grew like weeds, making 19th-century planters rich. That swath of fertile lime-and-marl soil, the Black Belt, spreads across central Alabama, starting just south of **Greensboro.** Among the 50 or so antebellum houses in this small town, **Magnolia Grove** *(1002 Hudson St. 334-624-8618. Closed Mon.; adm. fee)*, a shrine to fine southern living, has been open to the public since 1943. Features include plaster medallions, a cantilevered staircase, and original furnishings.

Southwest on US 80 lies **Demopolis,** "city of the people," started in 1817 by a group of exiles from Napoleonic France. Their grapes wouldn't grow here, but cotton would, and planters from eastern states soon began moving in to take advantage. An architectural masterpiece from those days, enchanting **Gaineswood**★★ *(Cedar and Whitfield Sts. 334-289-4846. Adm. fee)* reflects the refined and varied tastes of planter Gen. Nathan Whitfield, original owner and designer of the house. And overlooking the Tombigbee River, **Bluff Hall** *(405 Commissioners Ave. 334-289-1666. Closed Mon.; adm. fee)* is an example of a federal house converted to the more fashionable Greek Revival around 1850. It's not as elegant as Gaineswood but still worth a look.

Take US 80 east, as it cuts through a mellow landscape

Ave Maria Grotto★★

An hour's drive north of Birmingham, you can observe how much an artist can produce in 50 years. Early in the century, Bavarian-born Brother Joseph began collecting bits of glass, cast-off jewelry, marbles, and shells, and turning them into model cathedrals and shrines, Biblical scenes and famous buildings. The remarkable result is a landscaped city of miniatures tucked into a hillside at the Benedictine **St. Bernard Abbey** *(US 278, E of Cullman. 205-734-4110. Adm. fee)*. Brother Joseph finished his last project in 1958 at age 80—a 1/75th-scale Basilica of Lourdes.

Alabama River, southwest of Selma

of cattle ranches. Cotton fields here and there remind you
that you're not in the open-range West.

A lovely town of old houses and churches, **❻ Selma**★
has become known in recent decades for its civil rights
activity. Pick up maps and literature at the Visitor Center
(*2207 Broad St. 334-875-7485*), then drive down to **Stur-
divant Hall**★★ (*713 Mabry St. 334-872-5626. Closed Mon.;
adm. fee*). One of the very finest house museums in the
state, this neoclassic showpiece glorifies the Old South
gentry with its fluted columns and ornate ironwork, its
gold-leaf mirrors and elaborate ceiling medallions.

For an excursion into the country, go southwest on
Ala. 22 to **Cahawba** (*14 miles, following signs. 334-872-8058*),
site of Alabama's state capital from 1820 to 1826. Brick
chimneys and other ruins remain of the town that flow-
ered here on the Alabama River briefly during the 1820s.

Come back through Selma and visit the **Old Depot
Museum** (*4 Martin Luther King, Jr., St. 334-874-2197. Adm.
fee*), which displays an outstanding collection of planta-
tion-life photos; and the **National Voting Rights Museum**
(*1012 Water St. 334-418-0800. Closed Sun.; adm. fee*), a small
facility housing photographs and films relating to the 1965
march to Montgomery. As you leave town on US 80, you
cross the **Edmund Pettus Bridge** where the marchers
were rebuffed by state troopers. Two weeks later, led by
Martin Luther King, Jr., and protected by National Guards-
men, thousands of disenfranchised blacks set out on the
56-mile walk. As you follow US 80 east, you pass the cotton fields where they slept on the 5-day march, the same
fields their ancestors worked as slaves.

● **190 miles** ● **2 days** ● **Year-round**

Presidents, Civil War prisoners, and present-day soldiers have frequented the quiet fields and small towns of western Georgia. Little wonder, then, that this short drive through an unassuming country-side of peanut farms and red-clay hills passes a number of top-notch historical attractions.

Start in the industrial city of **❶ Columbus** ★ *(Convention & Visitors Bureau, 1000 Bay Ave. 706-322-1613 or 800-999-1613),* on the last navigable stretch of the Chattahoochee River. After decades of sprawl, Columbus has set about revitalizing its uptown area, converting older businesses into trendy shops and restaurants, and generally returning the focus of the town to its greatest natural resource, the river.

Begin your visit at the **Riverwalk ★ ★,** a landscaped 12-mile-long promenade favored by walkers, joggers, skaters, bikers, and sidewalk musicians. You can walk up to a good view of the falls that once powered the textile mills, then stroll down as far as you like along the river that separates Georgia and Alabama.

Massed along the river, the 26-block historic district is chock full of Victorian and other style houses with tidy gardens and wide front porches. The **Historic Columbus Foundation** *(700 Broadway. 706-322-0756. Tours Mon.-Fri.; fee)* gives guided tours that include a relocated log cabin; a house occupied by Dr. John Pemberton, inventor of Coca-Cola; and an 1828 cottage considered the city's oldest residence.

Out at Fort Benning, the **National Infantry Museum ★** *(Bldg. 396, Baltzell Ave. 706-545-2958)* displays a surpassing collection of uniforms, weapons, and other hardware from the 16th century to the present, including Scottish claymores and Nazi weapons (two of which were Himmler's).

Head north out of town on US 27 into rolling hills and farmland. This zigzag road climbs toward the town of Pine Mountain. But before you get there, turn left at **Callaway Gardens ★ ★** *(706-663-2281 or 800-CALLAWAY. Adm. fee).*

Envisioning a place "prettier than anything since the Garden of Eden," Cason and Virginia
Callaway opened the 14,000-acre sanctuary in 1952. A
5-mile scenic drive wraps a constellation of serene
lakes set off by lush plantings and sprawling green-
houses—a setting unlike any other in the Southeast.
Be sure to stop at the butterfly center, alive with a
thousand butterflies.

Now take Ga. 190 east through **F.D. Roosevelt State
Park** *(Visitor Center, 2970 Ga. 190. 706-663-4858 or 800-864-
7275. Parking fee),* a 10,000-acre mountain forest with fine
roadside overlooks, hiking trails, a swimming pool, and
horse stables.

Roosevelt came to the area in the mid-1920s after
hearing about the healing powers of local warm springs.
Stricken with polio and low in spirits, he was willing to
try anything. Whether the water really worked miracles,
or the rugged beauty of the surroundings relaxed and
inspired him, a change came over the young man. He
continued visiting the area until his death here in 1945,
while vacationing at the modest, six-room house he had

Butterfly at Callaway Gardens

55

Callaway Gardens, near Pine Mountain

built in 1932. Now preserved as ❷ **F.D.R.'s Little White
House State Historic Site**★ *(Off Ga. 85W, in Warm Springs.
706-655-5870. Adm. fee),* it is still furnished the way the
32nd President left it. Also preserved are the servants
quarters, guesthouse, and garage, with his specially

outfitted cars. Don't miss the 12-minute film with wonderful footage of FDR playing water polo with disabled children.

The town of **Warm Springs** *(Welcome Center 706-655-3322 or 800 FDR-1927)* prospered as a resort in the late 1800s and early 1900s but would probably have died out if not for FDR and the Roosevelt Warm Springs Institute for Rehabilitation that he founded. Tourists now stop to browse the many antique and craft shops lining the town square. For excellent southern cooking on the cheap, try the **Blue Willow Cafe** *(Ga. 85W and US 27. 706-655-2195).*

Follow Ga. 41 south through hilly farms and small towns, peach orchards and flowery meadows. Most of the towns are lackluster, but the road is uncrowded and scenic. Just before **Buena Vista,** turn right on Ga. 137 and after the Big Sandy Creek Bridge take a right on County Rd. 78 to ❸ **Pasaquan**★ *(912-649-9444. Thurs.-Sun. and by appt.; adm. fee).* When artist Eddie Owens Martin (1908-1986) inherited the family farm in 1957, he set about turning it into a fevered dream of colored walls, mandalas, totemic figures, and bizarre paintings. The yard became a wondrous temple compound with brightly painted stairs and altar, the house a studio for artwork and fortune-telling. Though the self-styled St. EOM (or "Bodacious Mystic Badass of Buena Vista") could not make a living as an artist, since his death he has become a recognized folk artist.

F.D. Roosevelt State Park, near Pine Mountain

From Buena Vista, head southeast on Ga. 26 and Ga. 228 to **Anderson-ville National Historic Site**★★ *(912-924-0343),* where almost 500 acres of fields and endless rows of headstones commemorate the misery endured here during the Civil War. The Confederacy's largest and most horrific prison camp interred more than 45,000 Union soldiers in its 14 months of operation. Short on resources for its own men, the South had nothing left over for the vast number of prisoners of war at Andersonville, and nearly 13,000 perished here of disease and malnutrition. The driving tour passes earth-works and other landmarks; a prisoner of war museum recounts the privations and escape attempts of soldiers in various wars. A new museum, scheduled to open in the spring of 1998, will honor all American POWs.

Across Ga. 49 is historic **Andersonville** *(Ga. 49.*

912-924-2558), the restored depot town where prisoners and supplies arrived by train. Attractions include an old farmstead, a log church, a museum *(fee)* of Civil War artifacts, and antique shops. Notice the monument erected by the United Daughters of the Confederacy, which eloquently expresses the deep bitterness of the postwar years.

Take Ga. 49 down to **Americus** *(Chamber of Commerce 912-924-2646 or 888-CSUMTER)*, a bustling county seat surrounded by pecan orchards and large cotton and peanut fields. For a splurge or just a peek, drop in at the 1892 **Windsor Hotel**★ *(125 W. Lamar St. 912-924-1555)*, an inspired concoction of Moorish and neoclassic turrets, balconies, and embellishments. The lobby alone puts most small towns to shame and has played host to such guests as William Jennings Bryan and FDR.

While Roosevelt was frequenting Warm Springs, a future President was growing up not 70 miles away. Drive west on US 280 through a flat, rural landscape to Jimmy Carter country. Stop at the **Plains Welcome Center** *(1763 US 280. 912-824-7477)* to load up on brochures and maps, then head over to the

Classroom at the Jimmy Carter N.H.S., Plains

old Plains High School, now the Visitor Center and museum for the ❹ **Jimmy Carter National Historic Site**★★ *(300 N. Bond St. 912-824-3413)*. Classrooms furnished as they were when Jimmy and Rosalynn attended school here detail Carter's childhood and rise to prominence. Live footage captures the excitement that gripped Plains during the 1976 election. Particularly impressive is the 1937-style classroom of legendary teacher Julia Coleman, whom Carter quoted in his inaugural address: "We must adjust to changing times and still hold to unchanging principles." You can also visit the 1888 depot that served as **Carter Campaign Headquarters** *(100 Main St. 912-824-3413)*, **Carter's Boyhood Home** *(Archery Community. Currently under restoration)*, and the **Marantha Baptist Church** *(148 Ga 45N. 912-824-7896)*, where the former President teaches Sunday school.

From the flats of Plains, follow US 280 west, then Ga. 27 into the red-clay hills of **Lumpkin** *(City Hall 912-838-4333)*, a town that refuses to give up. Though the soil is not much good for raising nuts anymore, and some farmers have turned to cotton, peanuts continue to be grown and a drying and bagging factory still operates. The town square, anchored by an 1895 neoclassic courthouse, is half washed out and half revitalized. On the south side of the square, **Dr. Hatchett's Old Tyme Drug Store** *(912-838-6924)* serves milk shakes and homemade pies in an attractive old building with ceiling fans and decorative iron chairs. While you eat, look around at the collection of antique retorts and medicine bottles. Another noteworthy fixture on the square, the 1836 **Bedingfield Inn** *(912-838-6419. Adm. fee)* now operates as a museum and is furnished in the style of an 1840s stagecoach hostelry.

It's always 1850 in **Westville** *(S of town on Martin Luther*

Providence Canyon State Conservation Park

King, Jr., Dr. 912-838-6310. Closed Mon.; adm. fee), a living history village of relocated and restored buildings. In its peaceful woodsy setting, Westville feels more authentic than some real towns. An anthology of rural southern architecture, the 30-some buildings here include an 1878 Methodist church; an 1845 doctor's office; and the Chattahoochee County Courthouse, where Jimmy Carter's grandfather and great-grandfather worked.

Bad farming created the fantastic formations at ❺ **Providence Canyon State Conservation Park**★ *(Visitor Center, 7 miles W of Lumpkin on Ga. 39C. 912-838-6202. Parking fee),* a series of 16 deep gullies eroded into the soft clay. Early settlers cleared the trees to make farms, and the ditches that resulted from their farming have grown to canyons up to 150 feet deep. Walking trails explore them, but for the best views of the multihued cliffs, stay on the rim.

Take US 27 north from Lumpkin to return to Columbus.

● **360 miles** ● **4 to 5 days** ● **Year-round** ● **Some mountain sites may close in winter, due to weather.**

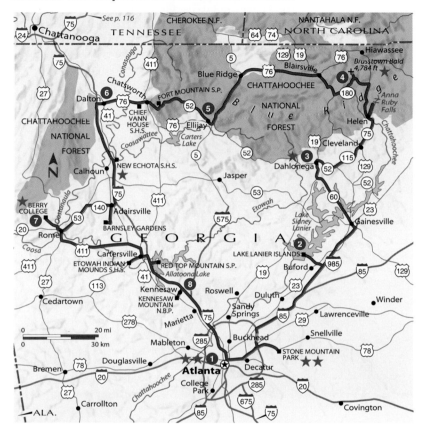

See p. 116

59

From the skyscrapers of the state's largest metropolitan area to panoramas from the state's highest point, this far-reaching drive visits much of Georgia's history and mountain scenery. Lying inland, the region draws a picture of the past two centuries of change. During that time gold has been discovered, the Cherokee have been pushed out, settlers have moved in, and Atlanta has burned and risen again.

The drive begins in the rebuilt capital city, with its youthful feel and tireless roster of attractions. From here you head for the hills, where lovely mountain lakes, rivers, and waterfalls await you. Along the way two charming tourist towns stand in the middle of Georgia's gold rush country. Coasting west through the mountains, the drive pauses at Calhoun, once capital of the Cherokee Nation; then visits the vast and beautiful campus of Berry College;

an ancient Indian mound site; and the site of a mountain-top battle that failed to stop Sherman's march on Atlanta.

For the past 133 years, ❶ **Atlanta**★★ *(Welcome Visitor Center 404-222-6688 or 800-285-2682)* has been reinvent-

ing itself. The sacked railroad center of the 1860s became the land of green-eyed Scarletts, then the financial and commercial Goliath of the New South and 1996 Olympic host city. Atlanta values convenience over charm, but if you search hard enough, you'll find a mixture of old and new, of big city glitz and southern simplicity.

Start in the the heart of downtown on Peachtree Street, where Atlanta's remaining old buildings hunker in the shadow of modern giants. Landmarks include: the **Candler Building** *(127 Peachtree St.)*, a 1906 pastiche of decorative friezes and stone busts; the seemingly two-dimensional 1897 **Flatiron Building** *(74 Peachtree St.)*, the city's oldest skyscraper; and the **William Oliver Building** *(32 Peachtree St.)*, with a showcase

Centennial Olympic Park, Atlanta

art deco lobby. In the midst of this brick-and-steel forest, **Woodruff Park** *(Peachtree St. between Edgewood and Auburn)*, with its 30-foot waterfall and music pavilion, bops with lunchtime businessmen, street evangelists, sidewalk vendors, and tourists. If you look lost, well-dressed "homeless" people are happy to give you directions. A cheaper alternative is to ask one of the official, pith-helmeted goodwill ambassadors you see on nearly every busy corner.

Continuing south on Peachtree Street brings you to the highly popular **Underground Atlanta.** This 6-block section of the old city was buried in the 1920s beneath elevated streets and readapted in the 1980s into a subterranean mall with historical markers, and 120 shops and eateries.

You're now about a block from the **State Capitol** *(Capitol Square. 404-656-2844. Tours Mon.-Fri.)*, brilliantly domed in Georgia gold. Tours detail the 1889 building, which contains a museum of minerals and fossils.

It's a short drive from here to the **Martin Luther King, Jr., National Historic Site**★ *(Visitor Center, 450 Auburn Ave. 404-331-3919),* where the civil rights leader grew up and preached. The Visitor Center has exhibits and a video presentation. Included in the 24-acre site are King's boyhood home, his church and gravesite, and the King Center that his widow, Coretta Scott King, founded in 1968.

To the south lies **Grant Park** *(Cherokee Ave. and Sydney St.),* with a **zoo** *(404-624-5600. Adm. fee)* and the **Cyclorama**★ *(404-658-1071. Adm. fee),* a 358-by-42-foot circular painting of the 1864 Battle of Atlanta. A huge revolving platform lets you follow the sound-and-light-show battle.

On the west side of town, the new 21-acre **Centennial Olympic Park** has lots of green space and landscaped plazas with sculptures. Adjacent is the **CNN Center**★ *(Techwood Dr. and Marietta St. 404-827-2300. Fee for tour),* which offers studio tours of Ted Turner's 24-hour news network. For a step back in time, visit the rambling Victorian **Wren's Nest** *(1050 R.D. Abernathy Blvd. S.W. 404-753-7735. Closed Mon.; adm. fee).* Joel Chandler Harris, who wrote the Uncle Remus tales, lived here, and the house is still comfortably littered with family memorabilia.

Drive north to midtown to see the fabulously ornate **Fox Theatre**★ *(660 Peachtree St. 404-881-2100),* a 1920s movie palace rich with Moorish and Egyptian details. Movies are shown here during the summer film festival; plays and concerts take place the rest of the year. About a mile farther north, the **High Museum of Art**★ *(Woodruff Arts Center, 1280 Peachtree St. N.E. 404-733-4444. Closed Mon.; adm. fee)* offers a fine collection of European and American art in a showplace 1983 building. Paneled in white porcelain, its four stories feature a bold, skylit atrium and huge windows.

For outdoor beauty, go directly east to the **Atlanta Botanical Garden** *(1345 Piedmont Ave. 404-876-5859. Closed Mon.; adm. fee),* where you can stroll amid dazzling floral displays and visit the desert house and tropical conservatory with its waterfall and carnivorous plants.

A short way north on Peachtree brings you to a midtown landmark, the castlelike

King gravesite at Martin Luther King, Jr., N.H.S., Atlanta

Rhodes Hall *(1516 Peachtree St. N.W. 404-885-7800. Sun.-Fri.; adm. fee).* Completed in 1904 by Atlanta's richest businessman at the time, the house luxuriates in such details as mosaic fireplaces and a stairway gallery of stained-glass panels chronicling the rise and fall of the Confederacy.

Atlanta's wealthiest citizens now live just north in **Buckhead,** a neighborhood of giant houses separated by rolling lawns and graceful shade trees. The city's finest restaurants and most exclusive shops concentrate here in Lenox Square and Phipps Plaza. The **Atlanta History Center★** (130 W. Paces Ferry Rd. 404-814-4000. Adm. fee) is the best place for learning city lore. The centerpiece Swan House, a neoclassic mansion, shows you how the very richest got by in the Great Depression; while the history museum houses exhibits on the Civil War, southern folk arts, and old Atlanta. A relocated farmstead and lovely 33-acre garden round out this appealing site.

Situated on the hill where Sherman watched Atlanta burn, the nearby **Jimmy Carter Library and Museum** (404-331-3942. Adm. fee) offers a good selection of exhibits and videos on the Carter presidency.

To explore one of the state's geologic wonders, drive due east to **Stone Mountain Park★★** (US 78. 770-498-5690. Fees for parking and attractions), a 3,200-acre recreation area capped by a tremendous granite dome rising 825 feet from the surrounding plain. Carved into one wall, the colossal figures of Confederate leaders Lee, Jackson, and Davis pay tribute to Dixie. On summer evenings a free laser show plays across the monumental sculpture.

You can ride a cable car or walk a trail that takes you above the smooth stone face to the mountain's summit. The park's **Antebellum Plantation,** a clutch of relocated buildings, includes a plantation house, an overseer's cottage, and slave cabins. Don't skip the **Road to Tara Museum★,** a wonderful collection of *Gone With the Wind* memorabilia.

Take I-85 northeast from the city to I-985. Atlanta has spilled so far into the countryside that after 20 miles you're still on a 12-lane divided highway. After that, things begin to soften and roll. Created by a dam on the Chattahoochee River, ❷ **Lake Sidney Lanier** is Atlanta's closest watering hole. The tentacles of land dotting the lake have been developed into a resort, Lake Lanier Islands (770-932-7200. Parking fee).

Continue north on I-985 to Gainesville, an unremarkable railroad and poultry center. You do pass a nice avenue of Victorian houses as you drive out Ga. 60 (Green Street) toward the mountains. Cross Lake Sidney Lanier and follow a route that snakes up past roadside fruit and vegetable stands.

Now dark mountains unfold in the distance. In 1828 prospectors swarmed into those hills looking for gold. A decade later, the Cherokee who owned the land were pushed out, and in another ten years the gold frenzy had shifted to California. People now flock to the town of

❸ Dahlonega★ *(Chamber of Commerce, 13 S. Park St. 706-864-3711)* to stroll the brick sidewalks and shop for gold and gifts in the stores around the square. Built at the height of the gold rush, the 1836 Lumpkin County Court-house now houses the **Dahlonega Gold Museum State Historic Site**★ *(Town Square. 706-864-2257. Adm. fee).* A film details the gold mining and minting history of the area and displays the picks, pans, and water cannon that the miners used.

Figures of Davis and Lee, Stone Mountain Park

Follow Ga. 52 and Ga. 115 up to Cleveland, then Ga. 75 past picturesque little farms and valleys to **Helen** *(Welcome Center, 726 Bruckenstrasse. 706-878-2181 or 800-858-8027).* In the late 1960s a group of local businessmen decided to turn their nondescript lumber-mill town into a tourist mecca. The result is Helen, a re-created Bavarian village of red-shingled roofs and cobblestone walkways. At **Charlemagne's Kingdom** *(8808 N. Main St. 706-878-2200. Adm. fee),* German native Willi Lindhorst has created a miniature landscape of north Germany, complete with autobahn, hot-air balloons, a circus, and trains.

On the south edge of town, the **Gold Mines of Helen** *(Ga. 75. 706-878-3052. Closed weekdays Nov.-March; adm. fee)* take you 300 feet into the side of a hill. Slaves started the tunnel with picks, gouging about 4 inches a day.

Follow signs from Ga. 356 up to **Anna Ruby Falls** *(706-754-6221. Parking fee)* in the Chattahoochee National Forest. The 0.4-mile paved Anna Ruby Falls Trail leads through a fragrant pine forest to the fortissimo rush of pounding water produced by twin falls, which drop 153 and 50 feet.

Now travel Ga. 75 north and Ga. 180 northwest and prepare to shift to low gear for the final corkscrew ascent (up Ga. 180 spur) to Georgia's highest point, **❹ Brasstown Bald**★ *(Ranger District 706-745-6928. Interpretive Center open daily Mem. Day–Oct., weekends in spring; parking fee).* Take the shuttle *(fee)* or half-mile trail to the top of the mountain. On clear days the 4,784-foot mountain—known locally as Bald Mountain—offers terrific views, and an Interpretive Center has robot rangers and exhibits on forestry, Native Americans, wildlife, and geology.

You can buy mountain crafts in small **Blairsville** *(Chamber of Commerce 706-745-5789),* then head west on US 76

Downtown Helen

through the national forest and take time to enjoy the views from overlooks. Continue on US 76 through the forest to ❺ **Ellijay** *(Chamber of Commerce 706-635-7400)*, a hub for outdoor recreation and the state's apple capital. As you push west on Ga. 52, flower-covered hillsides give way to steep grades and magnificent mountain vistas. Crest the ridge and you see the valleys and hills on the other side. In **Fort Mountain State Park** *(706-695-2621. Adm. fee)* you can stretch your legs on 14 miles of hiking trails or relax lakeside.

Entering **Chatsworth,** you'll behold the prominent neoclassic Murray County Courthouse. A few miles west of town, look for the handsome **Chief Vann House State Historic Site** *(82 Ga. 225N. 706-695-2598. Closed Mon.; adm. fee)*, built in 1804 by Cherokee chief James Vann. He and his three wives lived here until his untimely death in 1809; the house was later seized by the state government when Vann's son hired a white worker.

To the west on US 76 lies ❻ **Dalton** *(Convention & Visitors Bureau, 2211 Dug Gap Battle Rd. 706-272-7676 or 800-331-3258)*, scene of skirmishes prior to the 1864 Battle of Atlanta. In the early 1900s, townswomen revived the colonial art of tufting, creating a cottage industry that helped the area survive the Depression. They hung their colorful chenille bedspreads on lines to attract motorists. The industry evolved from spreads to carpets, and now Dalton produces a large percentage of the world's tufted carpets. The **Crown Gardens and Archives** *(715 Chattanooga Ave. 706-278-0217. Tues.-Sat.)* offer exhibits on the textile industry and the Civil War, displayed in an 1890 mill office.

Take I 75 south toward Calhoun and exit on Ga. 225 to **New Echota State Historic Site**★ *(706-624-1321. Closed Mon.; adm. fee).* Here in 1825 the Cherokee Nation set up a capital and attempted to fashion a government similar to the white man's. Their dreams of coexistence were shattered when the U.S. government forced them out in 1838 on a brutal westward march that became known as the Trail of Tears. You can tour the print shop, courthouse, tavern, and other restored and reconstructed buildings that stand as heartbreaking reminders of their struggles.

South of Adairsville, the ruins of an 1840s country estate form a haunting backdrop to **Barnsley Gardens** *(597 Barnsley Gardens Rd. 770-773-7480. Feb.- Dec. Tues.-Sun.; adm. fee).* The beautifully restored 30-acre grounds enclose a fernery, rockeries, a bog garden, and more than 200 varieties of roses.

West of town, Ga. 53 takes you south through gently rolling farmlands to **Rome** *(Visitor Center 706-295-5576 or 800-444-1834),* named for its setting amid seven hills. Follow signs to **Oak Hill and Martha Berry Museum**★★ *(US 27. 706-291-1883. Adm. fee).* Born to a Civil War veteran and cotton broker, Martha Berry (1866-1942) capitalized on her genteel upbringing to help thousands of young people. In 1902 she went from teaching Sunday school in a log cabin on her family's estate to founding the local institution that has been considered by some one of the country's best small colleges. Stop at the museum for an introductory video and a look at Berry's memorabilia; trails lead to the log cabin and the 1847 plantation house. A short drive off US 27 brings you to **7** **Berry College**★, an apparently endless spread of green fields and wooded hills. Though Berry claims to be one of the world's largest campuses, its 28,000 acres are shared by only 2,000 students. The nearby **Chieftains Museum** *(501 Riverside Pkwy. 706-291-9494. Tues.-Sat.; adm. fee)* tells the sad story of the Cherokee exile from Georgia and outlines Cherokee history and culture.

Head east on US 411 to **Cartersville** *(Convention & Visitors Bureau 770-387-1357 or 800-733-2280),* a railroad center since before the Civil War. The attractive downtown has a busy main street lined with shops and offices in turn-of-the-century buildings. The **Bartow History Center** *(13 N. Wall St. 770-382-3818. Tues.-Sat.)* holds exhibits on the Cherokee, the Civil War, and such colorful locals as gangster Pretty Boy Floyd. The **William Weinman Mineral Museum** *(51 Mineral Museum Dr. 770-386-0576. Closed Mon.; adm. fee)* has more than 2,500 stones and fossils, and a walk-through model of a limestone cave.

Scarlett Fever

Upon the publication of *Gone With The Wind* in 1936, an unprecedented literary excitement swept Atlanta and the country. The Civil War epic took Margaret Mitchell ten years to research and write. It won the Pulitzer Prize; the movie, starring Vivian Leigh and Clark Gable, took Academy Awards for best picture, actress, and director. The book remains the definitive portrayal of the Old South, and one of the bestselling novels of all time. The fanfare has been much less for the publication of Mitchell's *Lost Laysen,* a novella discovered long after Mitchell's death and published in 1996. Somewhat foretelling of *Gone With the Wind,* the tale of love and honor on a doomed South Pacific island features two male characters—one a gentleman, the other a roughhewn sailor—who vie for the love of a tempestuous, beautiful woman.

A few miles southwest from Cartersville, the **Etowah Indian Mounds State Historic Site** *(Off Ga. 113. 770-387-3747. Closed Mon.; adm. fee)* preserves several platform mounds built 500 to 1,000 years ago. A museum displays effigies, projectile points, and shell ornaments, some of them used in a trade system that linked villages from the Great Lakes to the Gulf of Mexico. East of the interstate,

Etowah Indian Mounds State Historic Site

Red Top Mountain State Park *(707-975-0055)* occupies a 1,950-acre peninsula jutting into Allatoona Lake, where you can hike and swim. Once a major iron-mining area, the park takes its name from the dark red color of the soil.

Continue south on I-75 to ❽ **Kennesaw,** where one of the Civil War's most dramatic episodes began. On April 12, 1862, James Andrews and 22 disguised Union soldiers hijacked a Confederate train and headed for Chattanooga. The train's crew gave chase, finally capturing their engine just short of Tennessee. The **Kennesaw Civil War Museum** *(2829 Cherokee St. 770-427-2117. Adm. fee)* houses the stolen *General* and exhibits relating to the event.

Two years later, William T. Sherman's army of 100,000 blazed a trail in the opposite direction, toward Atlanta. But they encountered a two-week delay west of Kennesaw, caused by Joseph Johnston's 60,000 Confederates. The **Kennesaw Mountain National Battlefield Park** *(W on Old US 41. 770-427-4686)* preserves the site of the June 1864 standoff; a road leads to the panoramic mountaintop.

To complete the loop back to Atlanta, take I-75 south.

● **260 miles** ● **4 days** ● **Year-round**

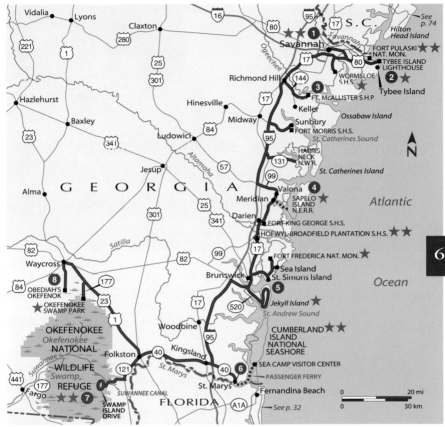

This Low Country meander explores a hothouse landscape of gnarled trees with tendrils of Spanish moss, vast marshlands dotted with waterbirds, the ghostly ruins of tabby forts and churches, and barrier islands preserved as wildlife and nature refuges.

Beginning in the aristocratic old cotton port of Savannah, the drive sidetracks to historic forts and the Tybee Island Lighthouse, then heads south through primitive shrimping villages. South of Darien, you visit a luscious 1806 plantation, hidden among the marshes, before continuing through the Sea Islands, with their mix of high-toned resorts and wild nature. The drive ends at Okefenokee Swamp, a 600-square-mile wilderness where alligators and long-legged birds lurk amid jungly backdrops.

Though Union Gen. William Tecumseh Sherman spared

Savannah riverfront

1 **Savannah**★★ *(Visitor Center, 301 Martin Luther King, Jr., Blvd. 912-944-0455),* developers in the 1950s nearly brought the city down. But thanks to the Historic Savannah Foundation, the city's architectural heritage and unique flavor were preserved. Today, nearly all of the 24 original squares, laid out in 1733 by colony founder James Oglethorpe, survive intact. An oasis of live oaks and azaleas, the squares slow the city's pace to a trot. Covering less than a square mile, the historic district, with its house museums and fine restaurants, is easily walkable.

A sturdy row of buildings arrayed along the Savannah River, **Factor's Walk** was the gathering place of the 19th-century city masters—the cotton merchants. The warehouses have been converted to restaurants and hotels; cobblestones still pave streets leading to the river.

Along River Street the "Waving Girl" statue honors one of Savannah's eccentrics, Florence Martus (1869-1943), who for 50 years waved a handkerchief or lantern at every ship entering port. Occupying a restored 1819 house, the **Ships of the Sea Maritime Museum** *(41 Martin Luther King, Jr., Blvd. 912- 232-1511. Adm. fee)* offers two floors of exhibits, including large-scale models of Savannah's greatest ships, maritime antiques, and navigational instruments. Five blocks south, the federal-style **Isaiah Davenport House Museum**★ *(324 E. State St. 912-236-8097. Adm. fee)* reflects middle class living in the early 1800s. By the 1920s, the house had become a rundown tenement. In 1955 the Historic Savannah Foundation was established specifically to save the building from demolition. The nearby **Owens-Thomas House Museum**★ *(124 Abercorn St. on Oglethorpe Sq. 912-233-9743. Closed Mon.; adm. fee)* is a model of English Regency elegance designed in 1816 by William Jay. Its raised first floor reduced heat, dust, and flooding.

Another William Jay masterpiece, the **Telfair Museum of Art** *(121 Barnard St. on Telfair Sq. 912-232 1177. Closed Mon.; adm. fee),* was constructed as a private residence in 1818-19. Now one of the South's oldest art museums, it boasts fine European and American paintings and sculpture. Just east, in lovely **Wright Square,** a marble monument tops the grave of Yamacraw chief Tomo-Chi-Chi, who negotiated with Oglethorpe the treaty for the land on which Savannah was built. The founder of the Girl Scouts grew up a block south, and the **Juliette Gordon Low Birthplace** *(142 Bull St. 912-233-4501. Closed Wed.; adm. fee),* an 1821 town house, is still cluttered with her family's Victoriana.

At the end of his famous March to the Sea, Sherman commandeered for himself one of the city's architectural gems, the **Green-Meldrim House**★★ *(1 W. Macon St. on Madison Sq. 912-233-3845. Tues., Thurs.-Sat.; adm. fee).* Built by a cotton factor in the early 1850s, the Gothic Revival house brims with exquisitely detailed marble, ironwork, and carved black walnut in its nine huge rooms.

The east side of Lafayette Square features the imposing Second Empire **Hamilton-Turner Mansion and Museum** *(912-233-4800. Adm. fee),* erected in 1873 by a city mayor. Now the residence of Nancy Hillis, depicted as Mandy Nichols in the 1994 bestseller *Midnight in the Garden of Good and Evil,* the house offers book, history, and "ghost" tours.

Drive east from the city to the impressive **Fort Pulaski National Monument**★★ *(Off US 80. 912-786-5787. Adm. fee),* an 1847 brick bulwark captured by Union forces in 1862. Cross the moat on a drawbridge to see battlements and explore dark tunnels. About a mile southeast of the fort the 154-foot ❷ **Tybee Island Lighthouse**★ *(30 Meddin Dr. 912-786-5801. Closed Tues.; adm. fee),* completed in 1867, provides spectacular views of island and ocean.

Double back toward Savannah and go southeast on Skidaway Road to **Wormsloe State Historic Site**★ *(912-353-3023. Closed Mon.; adm. fee).* A breathtaking live oak nave more than a mile long introduces this plantation built in the 1730s by Savannah colonist Noble Jones. A Visitor Center shows a 17-minute film and artifacts, and nature trails lead to ruins of the Jones's original fortified house.

Now travel briefly on US 17 south, exiting at

The Sheltering Sea Islands

Like a mother's arms, the Sea Islands cradle and protect surrounding marshlands from the brute force of the Atlantic. In these gentle backwater nurseries, oysters, shrimp, crabs, striped bass, and other marine life grow to maturity. With marshes quickly vanishing farther north, the islands also act as much needed rest stops for waterbirds migrating along the Atlantic flyway. Here they can stop, eat, and nest. Some animals make permanent homes of the islands—among them bald eagles and other threatened and rare species. So much wildlife counts on Georgia's Sea Islands remaining wild.

Richmond Hill for a 10-mile detour to ❸ **Fort McAllister State Historic Park** *(Off Ga. 144 Spur. 912-727-2339. Adm. and parking fee).* Located on the Ogeechee River, the Confederate earthworks withstood seven bombardments, finally falling to Sherman in December 1864.

Go south on I-95 and take the exit for **Fort Morris State Historic Site** *(7 miles E. 912-884-5999. Closed Mon.; adm. fee),* which defended the once bustling port of Sunbury during the Revolution. The devastated town recovered somewhat after the British occupation but eventually died as residents moved inland. You can walk around the fort's earthworks and trenches, or take a nature trail to gorgeous views of St. Catherines Sound and its rippled fringe of cordgrass. A small museum has excavated artifacts and a 12-minute film on Sunbury.

Possibilities for meanders abound at every exit off I-95, and if you head east on US 17, then Ga. 131 for 7 miles, you'll arrive at **Harris Neck National Wildlife Refuge** *(912-652-4415. Closed during hunts).* Its 4-mile loop drive offers views of marshlands with a tremendous variety of wading birds.

Continuing south on I-95, the drive turns east on Ga. 99 into a sparsely populated area where shanties and pickups hide in a swamp forest and all roads turn to dirt. At the edge of the community of **Valona,** a dockside seafood plant constitutes the area's sole industry. Follow signs to the ❹ **Sapelo Island National Estuarine Research Reserve**★ *(Visitor Center, off Ga. 99 in Meridian. 912-437-3224. Island tours June–Labor Day Wed., Fri., and Sat. Rest of year Wed. and Sat.; fee).* Boat tours interpret the ecosystems of this mostly pristine barrier island and explore the University of Georgia Marine Institute and **Hog Hammock,** a community of the descendants of Sapelo slaves.

Keep south to **Darien,** an 18th-century export center burned by Union raiders. Follow signs to **Fort King George State Historic Site** *(Fort King George Dr. 912-437-4770. Closed Mon.; adm. fee),* Britain's southernmost outpost in the American colonies from 1721 to 1727. The museum offers the standard display of artifacts and a decent 12-minute film; a trail leads to a reconstructed three-story blockhouse at the edge of a marsh of swaying spartina.

US 17 crosses the Altamaha River, dotted with shrimping boats, and continues south 5 miles to lovely **Hofwyl-Broadfield Plantation State Historic Site**★★ *(US 17. 912-264-7333. Closed Mon.; adm. fee).* From the early 1800s to 1973, five generations of the same family worked this graceful property. At one time the estate comprised 7,300 acres, 357 slaves, and

18th-century costume, Fort King George State Historic Site

numerous houses. The Visitor Center and museum has family heirlooms and exhibits on slave labor. A 1-mile trail winds under ancient oaks to the antebellum home standing on the marshes of the Altamaha River.

Gateway to the developed Sea Islands, **Brunswick** *(Visitor Center, US 17 at F. J. Torras Causeway. 800-933-COAST)* is a port town with lots of traffic and a couple of seafood plants. Most visitors skip the town and head straight to **⑤ St. Simons Island,** largest and most developed of the Golden Isles. Golf carts now crisscross a landscape where slaves

Hofwyl-Broadfield Plantation State Historic Site

harvested long-staple Sea Island cotton. At the island's south end, Pier Village consists of gift shops, cafés, bait-and-tackle stores, and a waterfront park and fishing pier. Two blocks east rises the 1872 **St. Simons Lighthouse and Museum of Coastal History** *(101 12th St. 912-638-4666. Adm. fee).* A 129-step climb gives awesome Atlantic and island views.

A causeway leads to **Sea Island** *(Visitor information 800-SEA-ISLAND),* a 5-mile-long spit of land occupied by a high-class resort. Designed in the 1920s by Palm Beach architect Addison Mizner, the Mediterranean buildings of The Cloister are graced by flowering plants and old oak trees. Guests have included Presidents Eisenhower, Nixon, Carter, and Bush.

Four miles north of this lavish enclave is the colony's first military outpost, established by James Oglethorpe in 1736 and preserved now as the **Fort Frederica National Monument★** *(912-638-3639. Adm. fee).* The threat these English colonists had long feared finally materialized in July 1742, when a Spanish force arrived. Oglethorpe's men managed to repulse the Spanish contingent, more than twice their size. Nonetheless, by 1758 the town was almost completely abandoned after a devastating fire. Today the townsite ruins are lush with grass and palms.

Go back through Brunswick and follow signs out to **Jekyll Island★** *(Welcome Center, Jekyll Island Causeway. 912-635-3636 or 800-841-6586),* which from 1886 to 1942 served as the preferred winter getaway for captains of

St. Simons Lighthouse and Museum of Coastal History

American industry. Stop at the **Historic District Visitor Center** *(Stable Rd. 912-635-2762)* for a short film and exhibits, then take the tram *(fee)* through the historic district and gawk at the redoubtable cottages of the Rockefellers, Morgans, Pulitzers, and Goulds. Craving peace and quiet, Joseph Pulitzer reputedly paid a local boat captain $100 a day not to toot his horn as he motored past.

In a region spread with gorgeous marshes, it's hard to say which is the prettiest. But the Marshes of Glynn, which you cross on the 7-mile-long causeway to and from Jekyll, surely rank high—especially at sunrise and sunset.

Take I-95 south then Ga. 40 east to ❻ **St. Marys** *(Welcome Center, 303 Osborne St. 912-882-4000 or 800-868-8667)*, a quiet waterfront town dating from 1787. Drive the few blocks down to the St. Marys River, where fishing boats dock and seabirds scavenge for scraps. In the early 1800s, smugglers and illegal slave traders flourished here. St. Marys now prides itself on being the home of the King's Bay Submarine Base. For an in-depth look at sub history, drop by the new **St. Marys Submarine Museum** *(108 W. St. Marys St. 912-882-2782. Closed Mon.; adm. fee)*, a two-floor facility crammed with models, artifacts, interactive computers, and, best of all, a 40-foot working periscope that allows visitors to scan the waterfront and nearby islands.

Cumberland Island National Seashore★★ *(Ferry leaves from St. Marys Visitor Center, 106 St. Marys Rd. 912-882-4335. Call for hrs. Reservations required. Fee for seashore and ferry)* is accessible only by boat. A wild and wonderful barrier island, Cumberland stretches 18 miles along Georgia's southern coastline, its marshes, forests, dune fields, and beaches sheltering shorebirds, armadillos, bobcats, deer, feral horses, and more. Thomas Carnegie owned most of the island in the late 19th century; the ruins of his 30-room mansion stand a short walk from the dock. Only a small portion of Cumberland remains in private hands today. Though there is drinking water at the small island Visitor Center at Sea Camp, bring your own supplies and plan to do some walking along miles of solitary beaches and quiet maritime forests.

Leaving the coast, travel west on Ga. 40 to Folkston, then southwest on Ga. 121 about 8 miles into an increasingly wild and open land. Turn right for the entrance to ❼ **Okefenokee National Wildlife Refuge**★★ *(Visitor Center at east entrance. 912-496-7836. Vehicle fee)*, a 396,000-acre tract of the primitive Okefenokee Swamp. When the ocean retreated from this area long ago, it left behind a dry, saucer-shaped depression that eventually filled with fresh water and mats of peat. Some of the mats have

Swamp Woman

Born on the edge of the Okefenokee in 1864, Lydia Smith Stone Crews was given a cow and a sow—and ended up a very wealthy woman with some 15,000 acres of timberland. Six feet six inches tall and 200 pounds, Miss Lydia cut a formidable figure, riding her property on horseback, her dress billowing and hat slouched. She could outwork, outwit, and outswindle any man or mule for miles around. As she herself said, "A man ain't living that can out figger me." Having outlived one husband, she soon took another: She was 64, her "Doll Baby" 22. By the time she died in 1938, Miss Lydia had long since passed into the world of swamp legend.

Cumberland Island National Seashore

grown thick enough with vegetation to constitute islands; smaller ones shiver like water beds when you walk on them. (A Native American word, *okefenokee* means "land of the trembling earth.") Stop at the Visitor Center for a quick look at the videos and exhibits and to pick up a brochure for the **Swamp Island Drive,** a 9-mile loop past stands of pine; a 1927 homestead; and a **boardwalk** ★ out into the swamp, where an observation tower rises on an extraordinary panorama of swamp "prairie" laced with lily pads, ponds, ibises, and cranes. To get farther out into the swamp, you can rent a boat or take a boat tour *(fee)*.

Head up toward Waycross on US 1/23, a scenic drive along the edges of the swamp. At Ga. 177, divert 5 miles south to **Okefenokee Swamp Park** ★ *(US 1. 912-283-0583. Adm. fee),* a private, nonprofit outfit. Opened in 1946, the park harbors a series of lagoons and islands, crossed by walkways and holding enclosures for bears, snakes, turtles, raccoons, and other swamp creatures. There's also a video, a 90-foot observation tower, and boat tours that thread narrow canals over black, mesmerizing water.

To see how swamp settlers lived a hundred years ago, visit the 20-some buildings at the restored homestead called **❽ Obediah's Okefenok** *(8.5 miles S of Waycross on Swamp Rd. 912-287-0090. Adm. fee).* Nature trails wander through 10 acres of marshes and woods, and cages holding more than 75 different species of animals.

US 84 will take you northeast back to Savannah.

The Old South ★

● **320 miles** ● **3 to 4 days** ● **Year-round**

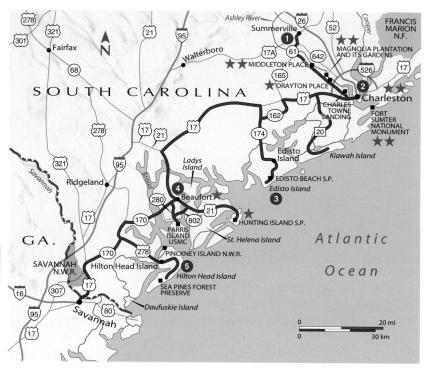

From Charleston to Savannah, Georgia, South Carolina's Low Country sings a gentle melody of broad grassy marshes and lush barrier islands that temper the southern coast. Historic cities and towns add a rich harmony to the natural landscape. Start your tour in the bustling town of Summerville, once a fancy retreat for those escaping the Low Country's summer vapors. Then take the Ashley River Road past three of the country's finest plantations, survivors of the Civil War. In Charleston, grande dame of southern cities, visit places of great beauty and historic import. Heading south on US 17, you can take coastal excursions that offer a look at developed Kiawah Island and more natural Edisto Island. Next, stroll or drive the quiet, shady streets of lovely Beaufort, capital of the South Carolina Sea Islands. The town's graceful old houses tell stories of war and peace from the American Revolution to yesterday's hurricane. Bridges and roads traverse islands settled by freed slaves and lead to an uncrowded state park that's half woods, half beach. South of town, stop by the Marine Corps Recruit Depot on Parris Island and the tony resorts of Hilton Head. From here it's an easy, pretty drive down toward that sultry southern flower, Savannah.

Rice planters began coming to ❶ **Summerville** *(Chamber of Commerce 203-873-2931)* in the mid-18th century to escape the oppressive, malarial swamps along the coastal rivers. Not knowing the connection between mosquitoes and disease, they thought the pines and higher elevation made for healthy living. Drive out Carolina Avenue to see some of the charming cottages they built. Main Street is a friendly blend of shops, restaurants, shade trees, azaleas, and camellias.

Take S.C. 61, the Ashley River Road, south through archways of moss-hung live oaks to the plantations facing the river, once their main highway. Boasting some of the oldest formally landscaped gardens in the country, **Middleton Place**★★ *(S.C. 61. 803-556-6020 or 800-782-3608. Adm. fee)* is the crown jewel of area plantations. Henry Middleton, whose son signed the Declaration of Independence, began the project in 1741. A hundred slaves worked for ten years to create a New World mirror of European elegance. Pathways wind past year-round blooms, and a terraced front lawn sweeps toward two wing-shaped ponds, presenting an unforgettable picture.

Antique shop, Main Street, Summerville

More extensive, though not as orderly, the profuse plantings 3 miles south at **Magnolia Plantation and its Gardens**★★ *(S.C. 61. 803-571-1266. Adm. fee)* make for a good half-day visit. As at Middleton, the original house was burned by Sherman's troops; and marble cherubs in the 50-acre gardens, begun in the 1680s, still show scars of potshots taken by Union looters. Built after the war, the current house, with its big veranda and stucco walls, looks more like a rambling inn than a plantation home; tours outline postbellum plantation life.

For unadulterated architecture, visit **Drayton Hall**★ *(S.C. 61. 803-766-0188. Adm. fee)*, the only Ashley River

Charleston, south of Broad Street

plantation house to survive the Civil War intact. Completed in 1742 by planter John Drayton (whose father owned Magnolia Plantation), the Georgian-Palladian house is a masterwork of symmetry and craftsmanship. Unfurnished, the house gives a sense of time's passage. Among highlights are the double staircase of hand-carved mahogany, yellow poplar molding, and a portico with sweeping views of the grounds rolling to a subtropical wilderness.

Charleston got its start in 1670 at **Charles Towne Landing** *(S.C. 171. 803-852-4200. Adm. fee),* across the Ashley River from the present-day city. The 663-acre park preserves the English settlement site, and 7 miles of trails lead past gardens, a native animal forest, and a reproduction of a 17th-century ship. Bike rentals are available.

Sweet-grass basket maker, Charleston

❷ **Charleston**★★ is *not* the quintessential southern city, because there is none other like it. Though new growth surrounds it like tree rings, Charleston remains Old South at the core. You can stroll or take a carriage past the colorful single and double houses, the neat gardens tucked behind lacy iron gates, the waterfront mansions with their gracious piazzas. Start at the Visitor Center *(375 Meeting St. 803-853-8000 or 800-868-8118)* for maps, information, and a multimedia show *(fee).* Then cross the street to the **Charleston Museum** *(360 Meeting St. 803-722-2996. Adm. fee)* to see exhibits on rice and cotton cultivation, slavery, and other Low Country historic pursuits.

Drive downtown and park in one of the lots near

Market Street, venue for many clubs and restaurants. The shopping district is along King Street; government buildings, churches, and inns stretch along Meeting Street. Off these two streets in either direction stand fine houses, large and small. The **Gibbes Museum of Art** *(135 Meeting St. 803-722-2706. Adm. fee)* maintains a good collection of Japanese woodblock prints, Charleston landscapes, and portraiture of eminent South Carolinians.

Two blocks east, the graceful **Huguenot Church** *(136 Church St. 803-722-4385. Mon.-Fri. March-May and Sept.-Nov.)* dates from 1845, the third church built here by French Protestants. From the sidewalk you can gawk at the ornate ironwork decorating **Dock Street Theatre**★ *(135 Church St. 803-720-3968. Mon.-Fri.; fee for performances).*

At the east end of Broad Street, a costumed guide beckons visitors to the **Old Exchange and Provost Dungeon**★ *(122 E. Bay St. 803-727-2165)*. A seasoned veteran of the tourist trade, the site offers two floors of interesting exhibits on city history, plus a dank dungeon where pirates and political prisoners were held.

On the sidewalks at Broad and Meeting Streets, African-American women sit under umbrellas weaving and selling traditional sweetgrass baskets. The city's grandest houses cluster on the end of the peninsula, south of Broad. (Their lucky residents are sometimes referred to as SOBs.) Choosing among the four houses open to

Fort Sumter National Monument, Charleston Harbor

the public is difficult; in each, reverential docents detail the history and inventory of the house as if it were holy writ. The stately **Heyward-Washington House**★ *(87 Church St. 803-722-0354. Adm. fee)* was built by a prominent rice planter around 1772. A federal marvel, the classy **Nathaniel Russell House**★★ *(51 Meeting St. 803-724-8481. Adm. fee)* was completed in 1808 for a wealthy merchant—highlights are the sweet smelling garden and the three-story, freestanding spiral staircase. The 1825 **Edmondston-Alston House**★★ *(21 E. Battery St. 803-722-7171. Adm. fee)* holds family silver, furniture, and other treasures; its high-ceilinged piazzas frame splendid views of Charleston Harbor. A flair for the dramatic shouts in every corner of the Victorian-style **Calhoun Mansion**★ *(16 Meeting St. 803-722-8205. Feb.-Dec. Wed.-Sun.; adm. fee),* an 1876 showplace with massive walnut doors and a ballroom ceiling that soars 45 feet to a domed skylight.

On the tip of the peninsula, the **Battery** (White Point Gardens) is an oasis of palmettos and live oaks, salty breezes, and memorials to the Civil War, which began out in the mouth of Charleston Harbor. Boat trips *(City Marina, 17 Lockwood Blvd. 803-722-1691. Fee)* will take you out to **Fort Sumter National Monument**★★ *(803-883-3123. Adm. fee).* In April 1861 South Carolina troops bombarded the fort for two days, forcing Federal defenders out and initiating the four long years of war. Park rangers now offer great tours of the site.

Leave the Charleston area on US 17 and follow signs

On St. Helena Island

south 17 miles to exclusive **Kiawah Island.** The last few miles are, as always in the Sea Islands, a soft prelude of spartina marshes and live oak passageways draped with cobwebs of Spanish moss. Developed by an Arab consortium in the 1970s, lush Kiawah has been decorated with golf courses, tennis courts, and villas that attempt to disappear into the landscape. Unless you're staying in one of the resort properties, there's no need to venture out onto the island; in fact, without a specific destination, you cannot pass the guard gate. Just before the gate, however, a road leads to public **Beachwalker Park** *(803-768-2395. Daily May-Sept., weekends April and Oct.; adm. fee),* with a boardwalk, umbrella rentals, and a snack bar.

Back on US 17, look for S.C. 162. For another

excursion, take this west to S.C. 174 and on to ❸ **Edisto Island.** The 36-mile drive tunnels through dense woods, interrupted here and there by a tiny grocery or shanty. After the Civil War, Sherman granted much of the Sea Island territory to freed slaves. The reservation-like system often spawned hopelessly complicated claims among succeeding generations.

Pick up maps at the Chamber of Commerce *(430 S.C. 174. 803-869-3867)* and head toward the oceanfront, where 1,255-acre **Edisto Beach State Park** *(S.C. 174. 803-869-2756. Vehicle fee mid-March–mid-Nov.)* encompasses salt marsh, live oak forest, and 1.5 miles of beach. The beach area offers palm-shaded picnic tables and bulletin boards with information on loggerhead turtles. A 4-mile interpretive trail winds through the marsh to an Indian shell mound.

Backtrack to US 17 and proceed south on US 21 to ❹ **Beaufort** ★ *(Visitor Center, 1006 Bay St. 803-524-3163)*, an antebellum Shangri-la of mossy oaks and fine old houses with double verandas and raised foundations. The state's second oldest town got its start in 1711. Occupied by British and then Union forces, Beaufort was spared the destruction of war and today claims nearly a hundred antebellum and pre-Revolutionary houses. According to tradition, British troops stabled horses in the 1724 **St. Helena's Episcopal Church** ★ *(Church and North Sts. 803-522-1712. Mon.-Fri.)*, and Civil War surgeons used stone slabs in the churchyard as operating tables.

Maintained in a 1798 arsenal, the **Beaufort Museum** *(713 Craven St. 803-525-7077. Closed Wed. and Sun.; adm. fee)* displays Native American and plantation artifacts and Civil War weapons. Maps, available at the Visitor Center, indicate the location of such landmarks as the 1834 **Henry McKee House** *(511 Prince St.)*, purchased by a former slave who helped capture a Confederate ship; and the **First African Baptist Church** *(New and King Sts.)*, built by freed slaves in 1856 and home of the Hallelujah Singers in the film *Forrest Gump.* Many inns and private houses have also served as locations for such movies as *The Big Chill, The Great Santini,* and *The Prince of Tides*—the last two based on novels by local author Pat Conroy.

Cross the bridge to Ladys Island and **St. Helena Island,** where the **Penn Center** *(Off US 21. 803-838-8563. Tues.-Fri.; adm. fee)* preserves the islands' African-American heritage with a museum of weavings, pictures, sweet-grass baskets, and recordings of the local Gullah dialect. The shady grove was the site of a school for freed blacks founded in 1862 by Philadelphia Quakers. Gullah 'n' Geechie Mahn Tours

It's a Loggerhead's Life

In a ritual thousands of years old, loggerhead turtles swim ashore along the southern coast during spring and summer, hefting their 300-pound bulks along the beaches in search of nesting sites. After laying their eggs in the sand, they leave. About two months later the eggs hatch, and silver-dollar-size hatchlings make a clumsy dash to the sea. Few survive. Predators scoop up some, the rest swim constantly for 24 hours to reach the Gulf Stream, avoiding hungry fish and birds on the way. They spend the next 20 to 25 years off the coasts of West Africa and the eastern U.S. But eventually the females return to the same region where they were hatched to lay their eggs. To help protect endangered loggerheads and other sea turtles:
1) Leave turtles alone.
2) Turn off lights shining on beaches—they disorient hatchlings.
3) Pick up trash; turtles may eat it and die.
4) Do not disturb nesting sites.

79

(803-838-7516. Fee) offers black history excursions.

Continue out to **Hunting Island State Park★** *(US 21. 803-838-2011. Adm. fee)*, a 5,000-acre preserve of maritime forest, salt marsh, and beach. You can climb the 132-foot lighthouse, built in 1875, for incomparable views of the islands and ocean.

From here, head back on US 21 to S.C. 802, and follow signs to **Parris Island** *(Visitor Center, Bldg. 283, Blvd. de France. 803-525-3650)*, home of the Marine Corps Recruit Depot; highlights include the late 1800s naval station, sites of early French and Spanish settlements, and huge fields where drill instructors bark at battalions of young warriors, making you very happy you're on vacation. The **Parris Island Museum** *(803-525-2951)* holds weapons, videos, homemade Viet Cong booby traps, and other exhibits presenting solid evidence of the toughness of Marines.

Take S.C. 170 southwest, crossing the Broad River where it slides into Port Royal Sound. Then follow signs southeast to ❺ **Hilton Head Island,** a barrier island again introduced by vast and beautiful high-grass marshes. One of the East Coast's largest islands, foot-shaped Hilton Head became a golf and tennis mecca soon after construction of the mainland bridge in 1956.

Hunting Island State Park

For those who prefer forests over fairways, there are some pristine spots left, including **Pinckney Island National Wildlife Refuge** *(US 278, after the first bridge. 912-652-4415)*, which encompasses 4,053 acres of woods, marshes, and tidal creeks on plantation lands once owned by Charles Cotesworth Pinckney. Some 14 miles of trails and roads traverse an island that is shared by ospreys, ibises, wood storks, and other coastal birds. Egrets and herons often pose in the shallows just off the causeway. Near the toe of the island, **Sea Pines Forest Preserve** *(Fee)* also offers trails through wildlife habitats.

The road down to the dreamy city of Savannah (see Sea Islands Jaunt, p. 67) cuts through a primitive subtropical forest. Much of the land is owned by paper companies and the 26,295-acre **Savannah National Wildlife Refuge** *(912-652-4415)*, a haven for waterfowl, deer, and other wildlife. A drive explores the mirror-flat marshlands, as well as the ruins of rice levees and slave quarters.

Columbia Circle

● **280 miles** ● **3 days** ● **Year-round** ● **July 4 brings the Lexington County Peach Festival (803-892-5207).**

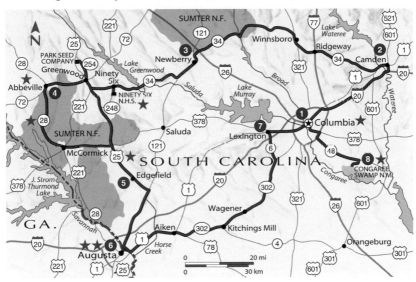

On this midland South Carolina ramble, you'll delve into the colonial age, touch base with the 19th century, and surface in the primordial past. The loop starts in Columbia—a small city with many excellent museums and historic houses—then heads into the countryside and past attractive small towns. Dipping into Georgia, you stop at the old cotton trading city of Augusta. An example of the Old and the New South, it claims a unique museum of southern art, a delightful riverwalk, historic house museums, and golf's Masters Tournament.

Finlay Park, Columbia

Then drive back to Columbia, taking time out for the Thoroughbred horse country around Aiken. The drive ends in the vast, untouched Congaree Swamp National Monument.

Laid out in 1786 where the Broad and Saluda Rivers mingle to form the Congaree, **❶ Columbia★** *(Visitor Center, 1012 Gervais St. 803-254-0479)* is a cinch to navigate by car—the gridwork of broad, well-marked, two-way streets makes getting lost nearly impossible. Travel by foot, on the other hand, is more difficult since the blocks are unusually long. During the Civil War, many works of art and documents were stored here, away from Charleston, to protect them from Sherman's incendiary army. But the general spared Charleston and burned Columbia, destroying most of the city and its treasures. The capital regrouped and today is a bustling city, though it tends to shut down early at night.

Opera House, Newberry

Bronze stars on the 1855 **South Carolina State Capitol** *(Assembly and Gervais Sts.)* mark hits by Union cannonballs. (Currently undergoing a 33-million-dollar renovation, the building will reopen in 1998.) A block away, at the edge of the University of South Carolina, you can visit the **Confederate Relic Room and Museum** *(920 Sumter St. 803-734-9813. Mon.-Fri.),* featuring military paraphernalia from the Revolution forward. Just north, the worthy **Columbia Museum of Art** *(112 Bull St. 803-799-2810. Closed Mon.; adm. fee)* offers works from the baroque, Renaissance, and modern periods; a planetarium *(fee)* presents weekend shows.

Columbia has four historic houses open regularly for touring; contact the Richland County Historic Preservation Commission *(803-252-1770. Closed Mon.; fee for tours):* The **Robert Mills House**★ *(1616 Blanding St.)* was built in 1823 by Mills (who came up with the original design for the Washington Monument). Across the street, the 1818 **Hampton-Preston Mansion**★ *(1615 Blanding St.)* was by turns the home of the prominent Hampton family, a Union headquarters, a Reconstruction-era governor's mansion, a convent, a women's college, and a boardinghouse. Two blocks south, the 28th U.S. President spent three of his teen years (1872-75) in the Tuscan-style villa now preserved as the **Woodrow Wilson Boyhood Home**★ *(1705 Hampton St.),* containing family furnishings. At the north edge of downtown, the **Mann-Simons Cottage**★ *(1403 Richland St.)* was bought about 1850 by a Charleston slave who purchased her freedom and walked to Columbia.

The first Secession Convention of southern states was held in 1860 at the **First Baptist Church** *(1306 Hampton St. 803-256-4251. Mon.-Fri.),* now dwarfed by a monstrous new sanctuary.

You could spend a whole afternoon at the **South Carolina State Museum**★★ *(301 Gervais St. 803-737-4921.*

Adm. fee), a trove of state history, technology, natural history, and art housed in an 1890s building that held the world's first electric textile mill. Exhibits include a display on local funeral practices, a laser science corner, and a transportation gallery.

Take I-20 and US 521/601 up to **2** **Camden,** the state's oldest inland town. Laid out in 1733 by order of King George II, the town found itself on the wrong side of royalty in 1780, when the British thoroughly trounced the Continentals in the Battle of Camden. Lord Cornwallis made himself at home in the **Kershaw House,** which was burned during the Civil War and reconstructed in the 1970s. It crowns the hill at **Historic Camden** *(US 521, just S of town. 803-432-9841),* a 98-acre reserve with several early 19th-century buildings adjacent to the old fortified townsite.

Then go west on S.C. 34, a winding wooded road through dot-size **Ridgeway,** boasting many fine Victorian residences. Continue on to **Winnsboro,** seat of Fairfield County. Much of the town was burned and looted after Union troops finished off Columbia in 1865, but about 50 antebellum structures remain. The 1833 **Town Clock**

Ninety Six National Historic Site

(Congress and W. Washington Sts.) stands across from the stout-columned **Fairfield County Courthouse** *(Congress and W. Washington Sts.),* designed in 1822 by Robert Mills.

Follow S.C. 34 over gentle hills and meadows edged with wildflowers in spring and summer, cross the muddy

Broad River, and dip into the farm and college town of ❸ **Newberry.** Driving the streets of this small town you pass dozens of well-preserved houses and churches from the 19th century. Stop at the courthouse green and observe the monuments, not just to Confederate dead, but to local soldiers of many wars. On the north side stands the five-story, tan-brick **Opera House** *(1201 McKibben St. 803-276-5179)* and clock tower, an 1882 Gothic structure. To the east, the circa 1850 **Old Court House** *(1109 Main St.)* is notable for its heavy columns and an 1876 pediment with a symbolic rendering of postwar South Carolina—a defiant game cock perched on an uprooted palmetto that a Federal eagle is attempting to lift.

Continue on S.C. 34 southwest through a pleasant countryside, where kudzu vines have turned trees into green dinosaurs. Two miles south of the town of Ninety Six, the **Ninety Six National Historic Site**★ *(S.C. 248. 803-543-4068)* provides a good picture of a frontier village in turbulent times. Supposedly named for the distance in miles to a Cherokee village in the foothills, the community grew to a major trading center in the mid-1700s. But within a short period (1760 to 1781), it was attacked twice by Indians and was the scene of two major Revolutionary War battles. The site concentrates on the second battle, a 28-day siege in which a thousand Continentals under Gen. Nathanael Greene attempted to take fortifications held by 550 Loyalists. They failed, but the British soon abandoned the wrecked village, and it never really recovered. You can take a 1-mile trail around reconstructed earthworks and the fort.

Back on S.C. 34 on the way to Greenwood, you'll pass farmhouses where flower baskets hang from front porches. To visit the gardens of the **Park Seed Company** *(864-223-8555 or 800-845-3369. Gardens peak May-Sept.),* a family-owned, mail-order business, take S.C. 254 for 6 miles north of Greenwood. A 14-mile excursion west of Greenwood on S.C. 72 brings you to the town of ❹ **Abbeville**★ and its quaint square and village green. You can poke into antique stores and a co-op grocery, get a bite to eat, or sit on a bench and admire the 1908 **Abbeville Opera House** *(Court Square. 864-459-2157).* Still in operation, the theater has played host to such stars as Jimmy Durante, Fanny Brice, and Sarah Bernhardt. Across the street stands the elegantly restored 1902 **Belmont Inn** *(864-459-9625).*

From Abbeville, you can take **S.C. 28**★ down through McCormick, then US 378 to US 25, heading south. Or backtrack to Greenwood and go south on **US 25**★ to

Edgefield. Either way, you'll travel some of the most scenic and least publicized backroads of the state. These durable, rolling farmlands have been worked for 250 years and are still verdant and lovely. Soft, grassy shoulders run to pasture fences entwined with wildflowers. Just outside **⑤ Edgefield** *(Visitor Center, 104 Courthouse Sq. 803-637-4010)*, the Long Cane Ranger District *(803-637-5396)* has information on recreation in nearby **Sumter National Forest.** Edgefield's perky little square—stores and town buildings neatly facing the central green and its war monuments—is classic small-town U.S.A. The county has produced ten state governors; the statue of one, subsequently U.S. Senator Strom Thurmond (born here in 1902), graces the square. Stop by **Old Edgefield Pottery** *(230 Simkins St. 803-637-2060. Closed Mon.; adm. fee)* and watch the resident potter spin out alkaline-glazed stoneware, a tradition in these parts for nearly 200 years. Afterward, enjoy a walk or drive around town; maps from the Visitor Center point out the many antebellum homes and buildings in the area.

85

Gardens of the Park Seed Company

More soothing scenery lies south of Edgefield, along US 25; in autumn sweet gums and maples turn the forest into a roadside show. Cross the Savannah River into Georgia and follow signs to **⑥ Augusta★★** and its **Historic Cotton Exchange Welcome Center and Museum★** *(8th and Reynolds Sts. 706-724-4067)*. An exhibit inside details the restoration of this magnificent 1886 Queen Anne and French Empire edifice. Also displayed are posting machines and a 45-foot market quote blackboard from the days of the original cotton exchange.

Walk behind the Welcome Center to the Savannah River, where the cotton was shipped that made Augusta the second largest inland cotton port in the country. A 5-block **Riverwalk★** takes you along the levee, built in 1929 after one too many floods. Or stroll along the lower walkway, under the shade trees along the river. In addition to the usual benches, colorful plantings, and information boards, this esplanade has several historical offerings. You can take a turn through history at the **Augusta-Richmond County Museum** *(560 Reynolds St. 706-722-8454. Closed Mon.; adm. fee)*, a big new facility with a Confederate field desk, a 1930s streetcar, a salute to the Masters Tournament, and other exhibits. The **Gertrude Herbert Institute of Art** *(506 Telfair St. 706-722-5495. Tues.-Sat.; donation),* an elegant federal house built in 1818, holds studio classrooms and galleries.

Overlooking the city canal, nearby **Meadow Garden**★ *(1320 Independence Dr. 706-724-4174. Mon.-Fri.; adm. fee)* maintains a sense of authenticity, even though it has been unoccupied for decades. Signer of the Declaration of Independence and U.S. Senator George Walton lived here from the 1790s to the early 1800s, and the house has a pleasantly unpolished, creaky feel.

The unique and distinctly southern **Morris Museum of Art**★★ *(W end of Riverwalk, 1 10th St. 706-724-7501. Closed Mon.; adm. fee)* showcases the art and artists of the South, from pre-Civil War days through the present. In one room hangs antebellum portraiture, while another shows historical images of African Americans. A contemporary gallery has oils executed by talented artists of the New South. Few places offer such a comprehensive and immediately accessible picture of the southern experience.

Augusta Riverwalk

Also worth a look is the 1797 **Ezekiel Harris House** *(1822 Broad St. 706-724-0436. Tues.-Sat.; adm. fee),* a gambrel-roofed frame structure built by a tobacco merchant.

Take US 1/78 northeast back into South Carolina and toward **Aiken** *(Chamber of Commerce, 400 Laurens St. 803-641-1111).* The route follows Horse Creek through a landscape peppered with little mill towns settled in the mid-1800s. Aiken's boulevard-style streets might present a challenge to motorists. Just remember that with wide medians dividing all of the streets, every street in town is essentially one way.

This is Thoroughbred country, known for its races, polo, fox hunts, and steeplechases. You can pick up a driving map at the Chamber of Commerce and explore some of the sandy carriage paths that border the area's lush horse farms and polo fields. On the way out of town, stop at the **Aiken County Historical Museum** *(433 Newberry St. S.W. 803-642-2015. Closed Mon.; donation).* Arrayed in a 1931 mansion, this impressive collection of community heirlooms sprawls through three buildings and three floors, and includes leg irons made by and for slaves, Victorian clothes, and a display on local kaolin mining.

Congaree Swamp National Monument

The nearby **Hopeland Gardens** and **Aiken Thoroughbred Racing Hall of Fame** ★ *(149 Dupree Pl. 803-642-7630. Gardens year-round, hall Sept.-May Tues.-Sun.)* are a must. Behind serpentine walls the 14-acre garden is an aromatic outdoor sanctuary of reflecting pools, bridges, fountains, and flowers, roofed by a network of deodora oak branches. The Hall of Fame spotlights the many championship horses that have been trained in Aiken. Across Whiskey Road, Mead Avenue will get you started on a horse-country meander.

From Aiken, wriggle the backroads home to Columbia, through open meadowland and fields of beans, cotton, and corn. US 78 and S.C. 302 lead you through Kitchings Mill to Wagener, once on the map as an Indian crossing and then a railroad depot. Beyond, make your way on S.C. 6 up to ❼ **Lexington** and visit the **Lexington County Museum** *(232 Fox St., off US 378. 803-359-8369. Closed Mon.; adm. fee),* a spread of late 18th- and early 19th-century buildings that includes three log cabins, a schoolhouse, a slave quarters, and a three-seater privy.

After you reach Columbia, end your trip with a detour on S.C. 48 about 20 miles, following signs for the **Congaree Swamp National Monument** ★ *(803-776-4396).* Designated an international biosphere reserve by UNESCO, this 22,200-acre swamp contains the largest expanse of old-growth floodplain forest in the country. Bald cypress, loblolly pine, tupelo, and many other trees have reached record heights and ages in this fertile forest. Miles of hiking trails disappear into that forest, and boardwalks will take you through the woodlands and across a swamp where gnarled cypress knees protrude from the murky water. You can also canoe, fish *(license required),* and camp *(permit required).*

Carolina Beaches ★★

● **280 miles** ● **2 to 3 days** ● **Year-round**

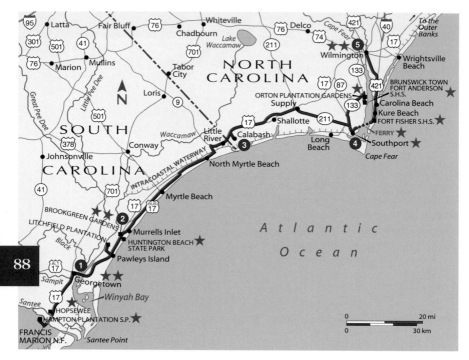

Bracketed by the two colonial towns of Georgetown and Wilmington, this easy drive will introduce you to the soft coastal landscape of the Carolinas and show you some of the most fascinating history of both states. From the defunct plantations of the antebellum gentry, to Civil War forts and restored town houses that preserve the elegance of the past, the route tells a rich story of failed grandeur. Along the way, you can visit an old-fashioned beach resort that has attracted vacationers for more than two centuries, as well as stop off at new resorts that pulse with modern excitement.

The heart of the rich rice-growing culture was

❶ Georgetown ★★ *(Chamber of Commerce, Front and Broad Sts. 803-546-8436)*, a seaport situated at the outlet of four rivers. In the mid-1800s, Georgetown exported more rice than any port in the world. More than 200 area plantations covered the tidal flats and swamps with rice fields (see sidebar, p. 92). By 1920 the rice era was over, but modern-day Georgetown maintains an air of humbled elegance. Just off the highway, old oaks shade wide, quiet streets where fine houses from the 18th and 19th centuries still stand with

shoulders erect. You can walk the 3-block downtown past
shops and restaurants or stroll the boardwalk along the
Sampit River, where fishing boats pull up to dock.

Stop by the **Rice Museum** *(Front and Screven Sts. 803-
546-7423. Closed Sun.; adm. fee),* housed in the clock-tower
building. This small but worthwhile primer on the rice
kings and their demise brings the past into focus with
dioramas, tools, and maps.

At Broad and Market Streets, **Prince George Episcopal
Church** *(803-546-4358. Tours Mon.-Thurs.)* was built about
1745, partly from import taxes on liquor. Aristocratic plant-

Hopsewee plantation, near Georgetown

ers and a way of life lie buried in its peaceful churchyard.

A few old houses and plantation manses in the area
now operate as inns, and a couple are open just for tours,
including **Hopsewee**★ *(12 miles S on US 17. 803-546-7891.
March-Oct. Tues.-Fri.; adm. fee).* Lovingly preserved over the
years, it offers an intimate peek at a typical planter's house.
Though the slave cabins fell down long ago, two kitchen
cabins remain. Modest in size by today's standards, the
two-story white clapboard dwelling (circa 1740) commands
a gorgeous tree-framed view of the North Santee River.

Travel a few miles farther south down a straight road
bordered by forest to **Hampton Plantation State Park**★
*(803-546-9361. Park open daily, mansion Thurs.-Mon.; adm. fee
to mansion).* It has a distinctly different approach from

Hopsewee. The house is grander, but empty of furniture.
Tours concentrate on architecture and construction and
mention such prominent guests as George Washington,
the Marquis de Lafayette, and Francis Marion. A gentle
sadness pervades the bare shell. Outside, the only sounds
are birdsong and the wind in the trees.

Backtrack to Georgetown and continue along US 17.
About 10 miles out of town, make a brief detour opposite
the turnoff for Pawleys Island. A few miles down Waverly
Road, turn right onto King's River Road for a look at **Litch-
field Plantation** *(803-237-9121),* an inn that was the 1750s
main house of a 600-acre rice plantation. A live oak avenue
leads toward the Waccamaw River.

Returning to US 17, continue north to ❷ **Brookgreen
Gardens** ★★ *(US 17. 803-237-4218 or 800-849-1931. Adm. fee),*
which boasts a comprehensive collection of outdoor sculpture that enhances the natural beauty of a property once
comprising four rice plantations. Gods and goddesses,
winged horses and mythical birds wrought by the likes of

Brookgreen Gardens

Daniel Chester French, Augustus
Saint-Gaudens, and Anna Hyatt Huntington repose amid 300 carefully
maintained acres of lush plantings.
The gardens, founded by Anna Hyatt
Huntington and her philanthropist
husband, date from 1931. Strolling
the central allée under a lacy canopy
of live oaks planted in the mid-1700s,
you can feel what the Carolina Low
Country was at its best—and still is.

Across the highway in **Huntington Beach State Park** ★ *(803-237-
4440. Adm. fee),* you can visit the
Huntingtons's rather unusual winter home, **Atalaya.** Though
from the parking lot the low-slung gray building with window grilles looks like a prison, it is actually a Moorish-style
residence with a palm-lined courtyard.

Prepare for a long, slow stretch as you come within
the mega-resort orbit of **Myrtle Beach** *(Chamber of Commerce, 1200 N. Oak St. 803-626-7444 or 800-356-3016).* For
over 50 miles—all the way up through North Myrtle
Beach—the highway begs you to stop for miniature golf,
water slides, beachwear, and ice cream. North Myrtle's
handful of new, high-gloss country and western venues
are attracting top-name musicians.

Gradually US 17 gets free of the resort tangle and
enters the pine-laden flatlands that stretch into North

Carolina. Once across the state border, stop off at tiny ❸ **Calabash,** famous in the area for its many seafood restaurants. At Calabash, US 17 leaves the coast and moves inland. At the crossroads town of Supply, turn east again on N.C. 211 and head to quaint ❹ **Southport**★ *(Chamber of Commerce 910-457-6964 or 800-457-6964)*. This town was a haven for river pilots in the mid-1700s and a major center for fishing and shrimping up until the 1960s. You can walk or bike down to the yacht basin and marina or along the shady streets lined with houses of understated charm.

Huntington Beach State Park

Stop by the **Southport Maritime Museum** *(116 N. Howe St. 910-457-0003. Closed Mon.; adm. fee)*, a fine little facility with an exhibit on "gentleman pirate" Stede Bonnet, who was captured near here; a collection of toys and other items recovered from a sunken 19th-century steamer; and a chronology of local history. A detour 2 miles north on N.C. 87 will bring you to Carolina Power & Light's **Brunswick Visitor Center** *(910-457-6041. Tues.-Thurs.)*, a gallery of energy-related educational fun. Continue north on N.C. 133 to **Orton Plantation Gardens**★ *(910-371-6851. Closed Dec.-Feb.; adm. fee)*, a languid Eden of azaleas and camellias, live oaks and magnolias, pools and lagoons. A path takes you through the gardens and past the privately owned house (1725), to spreading views of tall-grass marshes where rice once grew. Go south and you're at **Brunswick Town/Fort Anderson State Historic Site** ★ *(910-371-6613. Closed Mon. Nov.-March)*. An eerie

91

Myrtle Beach boardwalk

Carolina Beaches

Raising Rice

Outnumbering whites six
to one, slaves were the
machinery that made the
Georgetown rice empire
of the mid-1800s possible.
Adapting West African
techniques to the South
Carolina tidelands, the
men first had to clear the
cypress and other trees
from the soupy ground,
then build dirt banks, dig
ditches, drain the
fields, and plow them.
They planted the rice
seeds in the spring on
fields flooded with river
water, draining them out
through trunk gates every
few days to let the shoots
grow in the sun. Young
boys ran through the fields
beating pots and pans to
scare away birds. In late
summer, men and women
harvested the crop,
threshed it with flailing
sticks, and tied it in
sheaves. In the winnowing
house, they sifted the grain
through grates to separate
out the chaff. The local rice
industry struggled on after
the Civil War but could not
compete with Louisiana
and Texas. Hurricanes in
the early 1900s salted the
remaining fields, leaving
them again to the ebb and
flow of the tides.

stillness hangs about the ruins of the colonial port town
that thrived here in the 18th century. Malaria, hurricanes,
and attacks from privateers drove most residents to Wilmington; the British burning of the town in 1776 was the
final straw. You can wander past stone foundations and
over the earthworks of a Confederate fort.

Retrace your drive back to Southport and pick up the
Southport ferry★ *(910-457-6942 or 800-293-3779. Every 45
min. April–mid-Nov., every 90 min. rest of year; fare)* for a 30-
minute ride across the sun-kissed mouth of the Cape Fear
River. On the other side, US 421 heads up the Cape Fear
peninsula, bordered by the Cape Fear River and the
Atlantic Ocean. Just up the road, turn right for the **North
Carolina Aquarium at Fort Fisher**★ *(2201 Fort Fisher
Blvd. 910-458-8257. Adm. fee),* which features a 20,000-
gallon shark tank, a sea turtle exhibit, and a touch-screen
menu for your choice of films shown in a two-story-high
auditorium. The peninsula's **Fort Fisher State Historic
Site**★ *(US 421. 910-458-5538. Closed Mon. Nov.-March)* commemorates the site of an intense Civil War land and sea
battle. In January 1865, Federal marines stormed the
beach here under heavy fire and took the fort, shutting
down the last Confederate port. The Visitor Center has a
film and displays, and a trail explores the fort's remains.

Continue north on US 421 to the low-key resort town
of **Carolina Beach,** where a boardwalk and amusement
park complement the expected rows of T-shirt shops and
motels. The commercialism and development increase as
US 421 bends northwest to ❺ **Wilmington**★★ *(Convention & Visitors Bureau, 24 N. 3rd St. 910-341-4030).* Situated at
the confluence of two branches of the Cape Fear River,
the pre-Revolutionary town grew to prominence as a vig-
orous trade and political center. A Confederate lifeline to
the outside world, it was the South's final port to fall during the Civil War. A large historic district encompasses
street after street of gracefully restored 18th- and 19th-
century houses. Along Front Street are coffee houses,
antique shops, restaurants, and a microbrewery. Just
down the hill, cobblestoned Water Street offers upscale
shopping and eating at Chandler's Wharf and the Cotton
Exchange—converted 19th-century warehouse districts. At
the intersection of Water and Market (the main east-west
thoroughfare), a riverfront park has benches and a promenade. From here you can see the battleship **U.S.S. North
Carolina**★★ *(US 17 and US 421. 910-350-1817. Adm. fee)*
moored along the riverfront. The 728-foot titan earned 15
battle stars in World War II, for distinguished service in

Wilmington riverfront

such places as Iwo Jima and Okinawa. You can take self-guided tours through its maze of ladders and decks to chambers such as the sick bay, barbershop, and mess hall.

A couple of blocks from the river, **St. John's Museum of Art** *(114 Orange St. 910-763-0281. Closed Mon.; adm. fee)* exhibits Mary Cassatt prints, Jugtown pottery, paintings by Elisabeth Chant, and contemporary works for sale and show. Walk a block west and take a tour of the **Zebulon Latimer House**★ *(126 S. 3rd St. 910-762-0492. Daily May-Sept., closed Mon. Oct.-April; adm. fee)*, an Italianate town house with ornate ironwork and a refreshing fountain.

The nearby **Burgwin-Wright House** *(224 Market St. 910-762-0570. Tues.-Sat.; adm. fee)* was put up in 1771 by a merchant planter. The Georgian-style dwelling has double verandas, a back garden, and a basement that served as a Revolutionary War prison when British general Cornwallis occupied the house.

Two blocks east, recently restored **Bellamy Mansion**★ *(5th and Market Sts. 910-251-3700. Wed.-Sun.; adm. fee)* is a splendid example of antebellum architecture, built by a wealthy planter in 1859. Tours take in the four floors of the 22-room mansion. Continue down Market a few more blocks to the **Cape Fear Museum**★ *(814 Market St. 910-341-4350. Closed Mon.; adm. fee)*, a spiffy repository of local lore that offers a 350-square-foot model of Wilmington's waterfront during the Civil War, a sound-and-light diorama of the Battle of Fort Fisher, and a hurricane exhibit.

More of the beachfront area is visible on the Pamlico & the Outer Banks drive; see page 94.

Pamlico & the Outer Banks

● **340 miles ● 3 days ● Spring through fall ● Cedar Island Ferry (919-225-3551 or 800-345-1665. Reservations recommended)**

Exploring the state's oldest towns and some of its prettiest scenery, this eastern North Carolina route around Pamlico Sound ambles along two-lane country roads, crosses long causeway bridges, and hops ferries, without once passing through a town larger than 17,000 people. Beginning in historic New Bern, you travel north through a rural landscape to tiny Bath, the oldest town in North Carolina. After crossing Albemarle Sound, you visit the waterfront town of Edenton, then double back and head east to Roanoke Island, site of a 16th-century colony that mysteriously disappeared. On the Outer Banks, you'll see hang gliders and Windsurfers, climb a famous lighthouse, visit national wildlife refuges, and stop for a while on an island that still harbors the look and traditions of an old

Tryon Palace

fishing village. Finish up—and try to resist staying indefinitely—in one of the state's most charming little towns, beautiful Beaufort.

Situated at the place where the Trent and Neuse Rivers meet, **❶ New Bern★** *(Convention & Visitors Bureau, 314 Tryon Palace Dr. 919-637-9400 or 800-437-5767)* stood at the confluence of clashing beliefs between North Carolina Patriots and the British when royal governor William Tryon built his palace in 1770, putting the town in the political center of the colony. For a lovely stroll through time, walk the 6 blocks of Pollock Street from Front Street up to **Tryon Palace Historic Sites & Gardens★** *(610 Pollock St. 919-514-4900 or 800-767-1560. Adm. fee)*. Along the way you'll see a number of handsome old churches and houses. The palace itself burned in 1798; the current model of Georgian symmetry is a 1959 reconstruction. Costumed lords, ladies, and servants busy themselves in parlors and formal gardens, bringing the colonial period to life. Tickets include admission to the 1830s **Dixon-Stevenson House★**; the 1783 **John Wright Stanly House★**; and the **New Bern Academy Museum** *(508 New St.)*, with exhibits on New Bern architecture and early education.

Cross the broad Neuse River and head north on US 17 through flats green with beans, corn, and tobacco. Make a brief stop in **Washington** *(Visitor Center, 102 Stewart Pkwy. 919-946-9168 or 800-999-3857)*,

Bath B&B

a supply port for the Confederate Army. Though burned seriously by Union troops in 1864, the town still has a noteworthy historic district. You can also meander the old wharf and warehouse area and watch gulls and boats plying the Pamlico River.

A detour east on US 264 and N.C. 92 leads through open countryside to a forgotten pocket of the state. About 200 people claim residence in **❷ Bath★,** a 1690s settlement that became the state's first official town in 1705. Edward Teach, a.k.a. the pirate Blackbeard, lived here for a time after being pardoned by the governor. But Indian attacks, drought, and yellow fever kept the number of early settlers down.

People here like the quiet of their isolated little peninsula. Begin a tour at the Historic Bath Visitor Center *(207 Carteret St. 919-923-3971. Closed Mon. Nov.-March),* which offers an informative 15-minute film and walking tours. A crushed-shell path leads to the 1790 **Van Der Veer House,** which has exhibits on local history and archaeology; and the 1751 **Palmer-Marsh House** *(Adm. fee),* with its tremendous double chimney and original plank floors. Drive or walk to **St. Thomas Episcopal Church** *(Craven St.),* built of brick in 1734. Walk around the ancient cemetery and enter the church—a simple interior with brick floors and wooden pews. The silence is near absolute. On the peninsula's point, the 1830 **Bonner House** *(Main and Front Sts. Adm. fee),* surrounded by a white picket fence, claims the town's best view. Here Bath Creek caresses the shore, while cool breezes find their way through tall pines.

Backtrack on US 264 to N.C. 32 north. In about 30 miles you'll reach the 3.5-mile bridge that spans sparkling Albemarle Sound—the largest freshwater sound on the continent. On the other side, you find yourself in delightful ❸ **Edenton**★★, a 1722 town with immediate eye appeal. Like an oil painting of a perfect colonial village, Edenton embraces its bay with ancient oaks and double-veranda homes from the 18th and 19th centuries.

Tours of the historic district begin at the Visitor Center *(108 N. Broad St. 919-482-2637. Closed Mon. Nov.-March; fee for tours),* and wind around the town, stopping at various buildings: **St. Paul's Episcopal Church**★ *(N. Broad and W. Church Sts.),* completed in 1760, contains a 15th-century English brass chandelier. Magnolias 150 years old

South Broad Street, Edenton

shade old graves out in the churchyard. The **Cupola House**★ *(408 S. Broad St.),* built in the Jacobean style in 1758, features period furniture, exquisite woodwork, and a floor that has slanted so much over the ages you'll feel like you're on a ship. The 1767 **Chowan County Courthouse State Historic Site**★ *(117 E. King St.)* lords over a grassy green flanked by some of the most prominent houses in town, each with special architectural features and a bay view. The **James Iredell House State Historic Site** *(105 E. Church St.)* was the home of an associate justice appointed to the first U.S. Supreme Court in 1790, when Edenton was still an important port and cultural center.

Recross Albemarle Sound and follow US 64 east through boggy farmland edged by beautiful wildflowers spring through fall. A long bridge fords the Alligator River, and in a few miles look for the entrance to **Alligator River National Wildlife Refuge** *(919-473-1131).* A half-mile trail ends

Wright Brothers National Memorial, Kill Devil Hills

at a boardwalk and 50-foot observation tower overlooking a freshwater wetland. The 152,000-acre refuge supports wood ducks, alligators, and red wolves, as well as bald cypresses.

Just before Manteo, stop at **Fort Raleigh National Historic Site**★★ *(US 64/264. 919-473-5772).* England's first attempt to permanently colonize the New World has for generations fired the imagination of scholars and tourists. Settled in 1587, the 117-person colony appears to have completely disappeared by 1590, leaving behind only the letters "CROATAN" carved on a palisade post and "CRO" carved on a tree as clues to their still unknown fate. The Visitor Center presents artifacts and an introductory film on the colony, while out back stands a reconstructed earth fort, and nature trails loop past Roanoke Sound. *The Lost Colony*★★ *(919-473-3414. Summer evenings Sun.-Fri.; fee),* a symphonic outdoor drama that has played since 1937, also recounts the colonists' story. Adjacent to the fort, **The Elizabethan Gardens**★ *(919-473-3234. March-Nov.; adm. fee),* a vision of 16th-century England in America, offer an enchanting mix of formal and natural plantings.

In **Manteo** the newly expanded **Roanoke Island Festival Park** *(Waterfront. 919-473-1144. Adm. fee)* also deals with the colonists' travails. The park's signature attraction, the *Elizabeth II*★, is a full-scale, seaworthy representation of a 16th-century sailing ship. The 69-foot square-rigger carried 55 people, so personal space on those long ocean voyages was almost nil. Tiny downtown Manteo claims a couple of blocks of quaint inns and restaurants. Or you can eat where the locals do—**Doug Saul's Bar-B-Q** *(US 64/264. 919-473-6464),* offering a fine barbecue and seafood buffet.

Beyond Roanoke Island, you come to the **Outer Banks,**

Pamlico & the Outer Banks

Jockey's Ridge State Park

98

Jockey's Ridge

The state park preserving the tallest natural sand dune system in the eastern United States originated on a summer morning in 1973. Local resident Carolista Baum woke up to the sound of an earth-moving machine breaking ground for a new development at the foot of Jockey's Ridge. Although conservationists had talked for years of saving the dunes, no real action was taken until Carolista went out that morning and placed herself in front of the bulldozer. The "People to Preserve Jockey's Ridge" was quickly organized by the new Save Our Sand-dune group, and by the next year the site had been declared a National Natural Landmark.

a 125-mile-long chain of barrier islands that curve far out from the mainland, dividing the Atlantic from a chain of sounds. As the islands erode on the seaward side and build up on the sound side, they are slowly tumbling over themselves and moving west.

Driving along, notice the contrast between Manteo's quiet woods and streets, and Nags Head's busy strip of hotels and cottages. But as you go north on N.C. 12, you'll find development only in the towns, buffered by long stretches of pristine seashore, sand dunes, and marshes.

About ten minutes north of Nags Head on US 158, the ❹ **Wright Brothers National Memorial**★★ (*Milepost 8, Kill Devil Hills. 919-441-7430. Adm. fee*) commemorates the place where Orville and Wilbur Wright made the world's first powered airplane flight in December 1903. The site holds a reconstructed hangar for the 1903 glider, living quarters and workshop, model aircraft, and a visitor center where a historian gives a lively presentation on early flight.

Originally from the Midwest, the brothers went searching for an isolated place with strong winds, high elevations, and soft landings. The high dunes around here were just what they wanted, the gorgeous sunsets an added bonus—"The prettiest I have ever seen," wrote Orville. The dunes still make for good launches: At **Jockey's Ridge State Park**★★ (*Mile 12 on US 158, Nags Head. 919-441-7132*), to the south, hang glider pilots enjoy birdlike freedom. Kitty Hawk Kites (*Mile 12.5 on US 158. 919-441-4124. Fee*) can have you trained and flying in about three hours; the more adventurous can try boat-tow and aero-Ultralight flights. Or hike up the approximately 100-foot Saharalike dune and enjoy magnificent views of the coast and Roanoke Sound. A 1.5-mile interpretive trail courses through dune, shrub forest, and estuarine environments.

Return through the town of **Nags Head** (*Visitor Center*

919-441-8144). If you didn't bring your Windsurfer or kayak or parasail, this is the town for renting one and trying out the sheltered bays in the sound.

The drive continues down N.C. 12 as it threads through the **Cape Hatteras National Seashore**★★ *(Visitor Center, off N.C. 12 near Buxton. 919-995-4474. Late spring–early fall),* the country's first national seashore. Its 70-mile sweep of protected coastline extends all the way down to Ocracoke Inlet. The seashore's north end is interrupted by the 5,915-acre **Pea Island National Wildlife Refuge**★ *(919-473-1131 or 919-987-2394. Closed Mon.-Fri. in winter).* A nature trail here leads through wetlands frequented by herons, egrets, terns, and more. On the ocean side, look for the exposed boiler and smokestack of a Federal transport ship, grounded in 1862.

Traveling south, you pass an endless stretch of dunes and wind-pruned shrubs, with civilization represented only by a lonely telephone wire that connects with nothing for miles and miles. At any number of pullouts, you can park and go find your own acre of beach. If it's company you want, try **Canadian Hole**★, a big shallow cove on Pamlico Sound that's absolutely perfect for windsurfing, kayaking, swimming, and lazing.

Not far down the road, the much photographed 208-foot ❺ **Cape Hatteras Lighthouse**★ *(919-995-4474)* is the nation's tallest brick light. From late spring to mid-fall, visitors may climb the 268 steps to the top for breathtaking views of cape and sound. When completed in 1870, the tower stood a half mile from the sea, but by 1935 waves were lapping its base. Man-made dunes and steel pilings were put in to protect it. Now the plan is to move the whole structure—when funds permit—to the south, facing the sound. The light warns mariners away from Diamond Shoals—called the Graveyard of the Atlantic, because well over 1,000 boats have wrecked off here in the past 400 years.

Cape Hatteras Lighthouse

The low-key village of **Hatteras** has managed to hold back the breathless pace of development that afflicts many Atlantic coast communities. This is still a pleasant town without a lot of high-rises or traffic.

A free, 40-minute ferry *(800-368-8949. Every half hour*

May-Oct., on the hour Nov.-April) runs from Hatteras to **Ocracoke Island★★.** Pick up schedules at information booths throughout the islands. Each ferry holds only 30 cars and the wait can be up to two hours in summer. On board, get out of your car, feel the salt breeze, watch the trailing gulls, and enjoy the ride. The crossing affords brilliant views of the flat green sound, far out to where it buckles into the ocean.

Once on Ocracoke Island, most people pull over to look at the wild horses, descendants of the ones brought here by settlers or pirates in the early 1700s. At one time numbering 300, the herd now averages from 25 to 30 and no longer roams free.

About 10 miles farther along, across from the campground on the right, the **Hammock Hills Nature Trail★** makes for a peaceful diversion from the road. Plaques along the .75-mile path provide notes on pine forest and wetlands ecology; a platform gives views of long-legged birds dabbling in the salt marsh edging Pamlico Sound. What makes Ocracoke unique is its relative isolation and end-of-the-road feeling. Its fishing village, also called **Ocracoke★,** has sandy, shaded streets and a time-capsule atmosphere. The National Park Service's **Ocra-**

On Ocracoke Island

coke Island Visitor Center *(N.C. 12. 919-928-4531. March-Dec.)* has maps of walking tours that cover the picturesque, unpaved lanes around Silver Lake Harbor. Make a stop at the nearby **Ocracoke Preservation Society Museum★** *(919-928-7375. Easter–late Nov.)* and listen to videos and tapes of old-timers speaking in island brogue. Typified by phrases like "hoi toide," the dialect evolved from early 18th-century English coupled with southern speech patterns. You can still hear snatches of it in village shops, inns, and streets. Rent a bike or just walk the streets to absorb the island flavor.

To continue south on N.C. 12, take the **Cedar Island Ferry★** *(919-225-3551 or 800-345-1665. Reservations recommended; fare),* a 23-mile trip to the island that takes just over two hours. Unless you like vending machine food, bring a picnic. As you pass Ocracoke Inlet, imagine the furious sea battle waged there in 1718, when Lt. Robert Maynard took on Blackbeard. After the smoke cleared, the notorious pirate was very dead (five bullet holes and twenty-five stab wounds). Maynard's sailors put Blackbeard's head on their bowsprit, marking an end to the brigand's 18 month spree of terrorism along the North Carolina coast.

North Carolina Maritime Museum, Beaufort

At the ferry landing on Cedar Island, a concessionaire offers horseback rides along the beach. The drive down N.C. 12 passes through the wide spartina marshes of **Cedar Island National Wildlife Refuge,** interrupted occasionally by cemeteries and tidy little communities with wooden fishing boats docked in backyard inlets. From Atlantic, Davis, and Harkers Island, you can take a ferry to **Cape Lookout National Seashore**★ *(Visitor Center, 131 Charles St., Harkers Island. 919-728-2250)*, a 55-mile strand of wild beauty. The cape has no maintained roads and few facilities, only a couple of abandoned fishing villages. Visitors can camp overnight or spend the day fishing and shelling; bring a hat, shirt, insect repellent, food, and water.

Small enough to know in a day, beguiling enough to make you want to stay a week, ❻ **Beaufort**★★ *(Visitor Center, 138 Turner St. 919-728-5225 or 800-575-7483. Closed Sun.)* is a late 17th-century fishing village and safe harbor that knows how to pamper tourists and yet remain quiet and unselfconscious. The Visitor Center offers guided tours through several 18th- and 19th-century buildings. Downtown Front Street comprises 3 or 4 blocks of shops, restaurants, balconied 19th-century cottages, and a marina perfect for watching sunsets. Across Taylor's Creek, wild horses graze on Carrot Island.

Take a peek in the **The Cedars Inn** *(305 Front St. 919-728-7036)*, a 1768 white clapboard, now restored and operating as a hostelry. Two doors down, the **North Carolina Maritime Museum**★ *(315 Front St. 919-728-7317)* traces coastal history with fossils, model ships, decoys, an unsettling exhibit of beach trash, and an 1890s Life Car for sea rescues. Across the street, the museum runs a watercraft center where shipwrights build and restore wooden boats, and the fresh smell of pine fills the air.

To return to New Bern, take US 70 north.

The Piedmont ★

● **330 miles** ● **3 days** ● **Year-round**

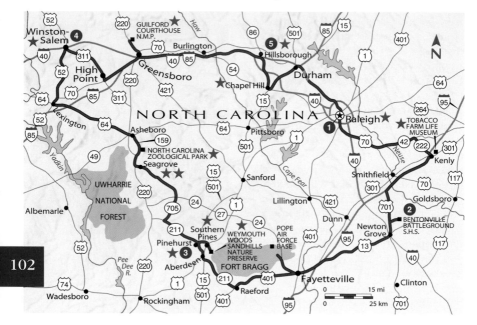

Connecting key towns in the heart of North Carolina, this easygoing turn through the state's foothill region offers more history than recreation, more subtle landscapes than spectacular views. As you move from site to site, you see less of the 1990s and more of the 1940s, the 1860s, and earlier. The drive offers a total immersion into North Carolina's diversity—from New South cities to an old Moravian village, from a world-class golf resort to booming university towns. Along the way, you can check out America's furniture-making capital, learn about the tobacco industry, visit the spot where Confederate Gen. Joseph Johnston surrendered, and eat a lot of barbecue.

The route takes off from the state capital of
❶ **Raleigh** ★ *(Visitor Center, 301 N. Blount St. 919-733-3456)*, a city loaded with fine museums and historic houses. Called "city of oaks" by it founders, it is still verdant with green spaces and parks, though it has spread considerably beyond its 1792 plan of 1 square mile. At the center of that original square, the 1840 **State Capitol** ★ *(1 E. Edenton St. 919-733-4994)* rises in Greek Revival splendor. Used until 1961, the former senate and house chambers have undergone recent restorations to return them to their 1840s look.

On the capitol's north side stand a pair of excellent

museums. The **North Carolina State Museum of Natural Sciences**★ *(102 N. Salisbury St. 919-733-7450),* which plans to open a new 7-story facility in 1999, presents live snakes, mounted animals, and the skeleton of a 50-ton sperm whale beached in 1928. The **North Carolina Museum of History**★ *(5 E. Edenton St. 919-715-0200. Closed Mon.)* features several large galleries with state-of-the-art exhibits on subjects ranging from colonial settlement to folklife to sports.

For more history, visit **Mordecai Historic Park** *(1 Mimosa St. 919-834-4844. Closed Tues.; adm. fee),* anchored by a 1785 Georgian house. President Andrew Johnson's simple circa 1797 birthplace and other relocated structures also stand here.

On the western edge of town, the **North Carolina Museum of Art**★ *(2110 Blue Ridge Rd. 919-839-6262. Closed Mon.)* covers works ranging from ancient Egypt to modern America. Included are paintings by Rubens, Monet, and O'Keeffe.

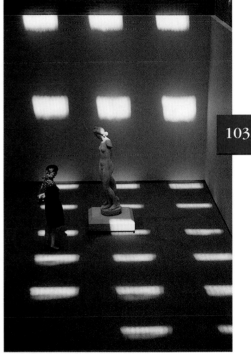

Take US 70 southeast to N.C. 42/222 east, a two-lane highway through piney woods and fields of beans and tobacco. The hills give way to flat ground that begins to turn sandy as you near the coastal plain. At Kenly's **Tobacco Farm Life Museum**★ *(US 301. 919-284-3431. Adm. fee)* you learn how flue-cured tobacco has affected every aspect of life in this region since the late 1800s. Exhibits detail tobacco grades and soil conservation, as well the social life, religion,

North Carolina Museum of Art, Raleigh

and education of tobacco growers. A video shows an auctioneer chanting at 500 words a minute, a practice very much alive in area tobacco markets today.

Now the drive heads south about 15 miles on I-95 to US 701 and the ❷ **Bentonville Battleground State Historic Site** *(910-594-0789. Visitor Center closed Mon. Nov.-March).* Here, in March 1865, Gen. William Sherman's army of 60,000 met strong resistance from Gen. Joseph Johnston's 20,000 ragged Confederates. Sherman's juggernaut proved invincible. The Visitor Center has exhibits and a slide show; a trail leads to Union trenches.

At US 13, head southwest through a rural landscape

Up in Smoke?

It was American Indians who introduced the world to tobacco more than 500 years ago. Since then people everywhere have been smoking, chewing, and snorting the pernicious weed, despite health warnings dating back centuries. North Carolina leads the nation in jobs created by tobacco, with some 50,000 North Carolinians involved in its farming and manufacture. About 5 percent of the state's economy is generated directly by tobacco, and 10 percent indirectly. Farmers who grow a variety of crops say tobacco is the one that pays their bills. Though it's more labor-intensive, it has a much higher cash yield—$4,000 to $4,500 per acre, compared with $101 for wheat and $691 for peanuts. Needless to say, Carolina's tobacco-industry spokesmen are always quick to forecast economic disaster whenever an anti-smoking campaign is underway.

stitched with cotton, corn, and soybean fields and dotted with shanties and lean-tos. The Cape Fear River town of **Fayetteville** *(Convention & Visitors Bureau, 245 Person St. 910-483-5311 or 888-622-4276)* has a few pockets of charm, though its downtown could use some care and a coat of paint. At the center of downtown the cupolaed 1832 **Market House** *(Green and Hay Sts. 910-483-2073. Mon.-Fri.)* has witnessed a lot of history, including the state's ratification of the U.S. Constitution in 1789.

The area's economy depends in large part on **Fort Bragg** *(Information Center, Knox and Randolph Sts. 910-396-2473)* and the adjacent **Pope Air Force Base.** For an in-depth look at "green berets" and other special-operations units, browse through the **John F. Kennedy Special Warfare Museum** ★ *(Ardennes and Marion Sts. 910-432-1533 or 910-432-4272. Closed Mon.).* Also take a peek at the **82nd Airborne Division War Memorial Museum** *(Ardennes and Gela Sts. 910-432-3443 or 910-432-5307. Closed Mon.),* which details the unit's history from 1917 to the present.

From here, the drive passes big cattle farms and small houses and trailers on its way to a speck of a town called **Aberdeen.** The town consists of little more than its Main Street, where you can shop for crafts and antiques; and a 1905 railroad depot, **Union Station** *(910-944-4787. Mon.-Thurs.),* where railroad memorabilia is displayed.

Just up the road, watch for golf cart crossing signs. A golfer's year-round paradise, ❸ **Pinehurst** ★ *(Convention & Visitors Bureau, 1480 US 15/501. 910-692-3330)* claims about 40 courses designed by the likes of Robert Trent Jones, Arnold Palmer, and Jack Nicklaus. Started as a resort in 1895, the small town has remained true to its roots—the business district, with its magnolias and clipped greenery, its bright white buildings and verandas, has the clubby refinement of a hotel complex. The pine-bordered Midland Road (N.C. 2) leads 5 miles to its sister town of **Southern Pines** ★, which has a somewhat more established feel.

To get a sense of what was here long before the condos and plush fairways, follow signs to **Weymouth Woods Sandhills Nature Preserve** ★ *(Visitor Center, 1024 Fort Bragg Rd. 910-692-2167).* Though logging in the 19th and early 20th centuries wiped out almost all the virgin longleaf pine forest in the Southeast, a slice remains here and there. Weymouth preserves a 525-acre tract, with some 400-year-old trees. More than 4 miles of needle-strewn trails offer quiet, except for the occasional sound of bomb practice at Fort Bragg.

Northwest of Pinehurst, the land turns hilly again with

Pinehurst golf course

rolling farms and meadows. Travel N.C. 211 to N.C. 705 toward **Seagrove**★★ *(Information Center, N.C. 705. 910-873-7887. Closed Sun.)* and stop off at some of the 80 or so potteries scattered along a 20-mile stretch. High-quality local clay has made pottery a tradition in this area since the late 1600s. Each place offers something different: **Owens Pottery** has a simple showroom and a dark, mud-spattered workplace where you can watch fourth-generation craftsmen turn out stoneware and earthenware. Just up the road, highly acclaimed **Ben Owen Pottery** (a distant relation) has an artsy display room with track lighting. The **Wild Rose** is run by a young couple who turned an 1859 log house into a cozy hideaway and filled its nooks and niches with their work. **Phil Morgan** offers difficult-to-make, high-luster pieces with a crystalline glaze. The only food for miles around is in the town of Seagrove—plan accordingly. **Jugtown Cafe** *(US 220. 910-873-8292)* is your best bet for country fare.

Seagrove potter at work

Take N.C. 159 north toward Asheboro, where the **North Carolina Zoological Park**★ *(4401 Zoo Pkwy. 910-879-7000. Adm. fee)* covers a vast 1,500 acres—about a third of it developed. The Africa section has nine areas, including a delightful aviary with some 100 exotic birds and a 39-acre grassland that is home to gemsbok and elephant, among others. The North America region includes a polar bear enclosure and the highly popular Alaskan seabird environment, where puffins leap off a 28-foot cliff into a pool.

Take US 64 to **Lexington** and sample what is arguably the state's favorite food, pit-cooked barbecue, at one of the many area eateries. Then continue on US 52 to ❹ **Winston-Salem**★ *(Visitor Center, 601 N. Cherry St. 910-777-3796 or 800-331-7018)*, a city born on the back of a Moravian settlement and raised on tobacco, textiles, and furniture. The Moravians, originally from Czechoslovakia, came to America in the 1700s and built "congregation towns" like Salem, with the church as the sole landowner. A remarkably preserved and restored village, **Old Salem**★★ *(Old Salem Rd. 910-721-7300 or 800-441-5305. Adm. fee to buildings)* captures the essence of that 1760s community. Houses with tidily swept yards and kitchen gardens alternate with trade shops and orchards, worked by women in *hauben* (bonnets) and men in vests. You can nose around the bakery and buy Moravian sugar cakes and ginger cookies, peek into a schoolhouse, listen to tolling church bells, watch a shoemaker, and dine (or spend the night) at the 1784 Salem Tavern.

At Old Salem's **Museum of Early Southern Decorative Arts** *(924 S. Main St. 910-721-7360. Adm. fee)* guided tours lead through more than 20 period rooms, ranging from the 17th to 19th centuries and displaying a collection of regional textiles, paintings, ceramics, and metal.

To see how the city has thrived in the 20th century, take the plant tour of the **R. J. Reynolds Tobacco Company**★ *(Whitaker Park, 1100 Reynolds Blvd. 910-741-5718. Mon.-Fri.)*. Located just a few miles from where Reynolds started making chewing tobacco in 1875, the plant offers a fascinating glimpse at cutting-edge mass production. In a spotless, bright assembly room watch robots and humans working together to roll out 8,000 cigarettes a minute. The 30-minute tour concludes with a sample pack for adults and a museum highlighting tobacco advertising and industry issues.

Tobacco was very good to Mr. Reynolds, as you can see for yourself at **Reynolda House, Museum of American Art**★ *(2250 Reynolda Rd. 910-725-5325. Closed Mon.; adm. fee)*. His 1917 country home is filled with masterpieces of American art by John Singleton Copley, Frederic Church, Jasper Johns, and others. The house features a two-story living room with a cantilevered balcony and a 2,500-pipe organ hidden behind Flemish tapestries.

It Ain't Barbecue

One of the few things guaranteed to anger a native North Carolinian is to serve him a messy plate of shredded meat slathered in tomato sauce and call it barbecue. It has to be pork, slow cooked in a pit over hickory wood, chopped or sliced, *lightly* seasoned with vinegar, ketchup, salt, sugar, and three kinds of pepper, and served with hush puppies, barbecue slaw, and sweet ice tea. The little town of Lexington can lay claim to being barbecue heaven, with 18 fine barbecue places and the annual October Barbecue Festival, which includes a Parade-of-Pigs.

106

There's also an indoor pool, a bowling alley, and a lovely English country garden on the grounds.

After escaping the city's tangle of highways, head south on US 311 to **High Point** *(Convention & Visitors Bureau, 300 S. Main St. 910-884-5255)*. With more than 125 furniture plants, the city sits at the top of the U.S. home-furnishings industry. Some 70,000 people from all over the world attend the city's biannual trade shows. The **Furniture Discovery Center**★★ *(101 W. Green Dr. 910 887 3876. Closed Mon. Nov.-March; adm. fee)* may not sound like the world's most exciting place, but it is in fact a top-drawer museum that takes you step-by-step through the construction of things you use every day. You follow a Queen Anne highboy from the gleam in a designer's eye to proto-type to finished product. Along the way you play with stuff on a designer's messy worktable, learn about ergonomics and wood, see a machine that can carve multiple pieces of wood at once, and design furniture on a computer.

Lexington Barbecue, in Lexington

Just beyond **Greensboro** *(Convention & Visitors Bureau, 317 S. Greene St. 910-274-2282 or 800-344-2282),* you can visit the place where Gen. Nathanael Greene's Patriots fought valiantly against Gen. Charles Cornwallis's better trained redcoats at **Guilford Courthouse National Military Park**★ *(Off US 220. 910-288-1776)*. A 2.3-mile loop road and walking trails lead through the battlefield. A good bet for downtown, the **Greensboro Historical Museum**★ *(130 Summit Ave. 910-373-2043. Closed Mon.)* houses two vast floors with exhibits on First Lady Dolley Madison, short story writer O Henry, the Woolworth lunch-counter sit-ins during the 1960s civil rights struggle, and other regional events. The nearby Elm Street commercial district has buildings dating from the late 1800s.

The drive next stops in the quaint, historic town of ❺ **Hillsborough**★, scene of much Revolutionary War activity. Six Patriots were hanged here in 1771; ten years later Cornwallis raised the British flag in front of the courthouse. Shortly after that, North Carolina Patriots captured the royal governor here. A number of 18th- and 19th-century buildings remain, including the **Alexander Dickson House** *(150 E. King St. 919-732-7741),* a late 18th-century frame cottage that now functions as the Visitor Center; the 1845 **Old Orange County Courthouse** *(E. King and Churton Sts.);* and the 1803 **Ruffin-Rouhlac House** *(101 E. Orange St. 919-732-2104 ext. 228. Mon.-Fri.),* which serves as the town hall. The **Orange County Historical Museum** *(201 N. Churton St. 919-732-2201. Closed Mon.)* covers local history from 1680 to 1865. At the 1759 **Colonial Inn** *(153 W. King St. 919-732-2461. Closed Mon.),* you can sit on veranda rockers and smell the enticing aromas of North Carolina barbecue, sugar-cured ham with raisin sauce, and peach cobbler wafting from the restaurant.

Take N.C. 86 through a bucolic landscape down to the university town of **Chapel Hill**★ *(Welcome Center, W. Franklin St. 919-929-9700. Tues.-Sat.).* The first state university in the nation, the **University of North Carolina at Chapel Hill**★ opened its doors in 1795. Start your tour at the Visitor Center *(Via Franklin St. entrance. 919-962-1630. Mon.- Fri.)* in the

The Old Well, University of North Carolina at Chapel Hill

Morehead Planetarium Building★ *(919-962-1236),* where you can also see superb shows of the simulated heavens. Later, take some time to stroll the lush campus. Don't miss the **Coker Arboretum**★ and its 200-foot wisteria arbor.

Just east of the planetarium stand the Gothic Revival **Chapel of the Cross,** dating from 1848; the 1907 university president's house; and other elegant old houses used by professors both past and present.

A visit to Chapel Hill would be incomplete without a walk down **Franklin Street★,** the gathering place for students and townspeople. Here you'll find the usual university contingent of cool coffee shops and bistros, stores, a theater, and restaurants. A tradition since 1948, the **Ramshead Rathskeller** *(Amber Alley, off Franklin St. 919-942-5158)* is an inviting Old World-style pub with heavy wood booths and dim lighting.

On the fringe of the south campus, the **Dean E. Smith Center** *(Skipper Bowles Dr. 919-962-7777. Mon.-Fri., closed for special events)* has 3,000 square feet for displaying mementos and highlight tapes of Michael Jordan and other UNC sports heroes.

A short drive up US 15/501 brings you to **Durham** *(Convention & Visitors Bureau, 101 E. Morgan St. 919-687-0288 or 800-446-8604. Mon.-Fri.),* home of **Duke University** *(Visitor Information at Bryan University Center, off Science Dr. 919-684-2323).* Graduates of UNC say that Duke looks out of place here, like Princeton suddenly sprung to life in the North Carolina Piedmont. The Gothic-style buildings of the West Campus date from 1925, when tobacco tycoon James B. Duke decided he wanted to build a university. The area centers around the impressive **Duke University Chapel★** *(919-684-2572),* a textbook English Gothic church with a 210-foot tower and magnificent stone carvings. The ten sculptures in the portal include Martin Luther, Thomas Jefferson, and Robert E. Lee. A quick walk brings you to the **Sarah P. Duke Gardens★** *(919-684-3698),* an orderly 55 acres with coolly intellectual green sweeps, brilliant flowers, and serene ponds.

Off campus at the **Duke Homestead State Historic Site & Tobacco Museum★** *(2828 Duke Homestead Rd. 919-477-5498. Closed Mon. Nov.-March),* you can learn more about the golden weed. The 1852 homestead belonged to pioneering tobacco entrepreneur and Confederate veteran Washington Duke, father of James. An excellent museum of tobacco history has antique packaging machines, cigarette dispensers, and auction videos.

The nearby **Bennett Place State Historic Site★** *(4409 Bennett Memorial Rd. 919-383-4345. Closed Mon. Nov.-March)* memorializes the place where North Carolina's Civil War ended. Here, on April 26, 1865—17 days after Lee's surrender at Appomattox—Joe Johnston surrendered to Sherman. The farmhouse, kitchen, and smokehouse are reminders of how momentous events can happen in unexpected places.

US 70 will bring you back to Raleigh.

The Smokies ★

● **343 miles** ● **3 to 4 days** ● **Year-round**

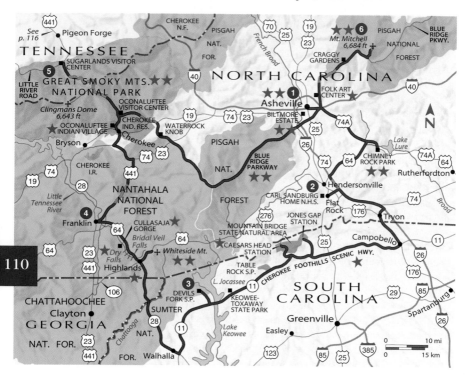

See p. 116

This loop through western North Carolina begins in Asheville, crosses the eastern Continental Divide, and makes a stop at the home of poet Carl Sandburg before dipping into South Carolina along a quiet road studded by a string of state parks. After a zigzag climb to the resort town of Highlands and through a gem-mining area, you'll pull into Cherokee, where tourism and Native American heritage coexist. The adjacent Great Smoky Mountains National Park offers a fine excursion before you take to the Blue Ridge Parkway for a long, spectacular drive over the Appalachians, climaxing at the highest peak in the eastern U.S.

Since the late 1800s, tourists have been coming to ❶ **Asheville** ★★ *(Convention & Visitors Bureau 704-258-6101 or 800-257-1300)* for its mountain air and outdoor recreation. But only in the past decade or so has the town acquired a reputation as a southern bohemia. Coffee houses, bookshops, and craft stores give an easygoing feel to the tree-lined downtown streets.

Biltmore Estate, Asheville

At **The Thomas Wolfe Memorial State Historic Site** ★★ *(Visitor Center, 52 N. Market St. 704-253-8304. Closed Mon. Nov.- March; adm. fee)*, you can tour the childhood home of Asheville's most famous bohemian, the author of the powerful 1929 classic *Look Homeward, Angel*. The late 19th-century boardinghouse run by his mother was the setting for the novel, as well as for several of Wolfe's short stories. A few blocks away, **Pack Place Education, Arts, & Science Center** *(2 S. Pack Sq. 704-257-4500. Tues.-Sat. year-round, Sun. June-Oct.; adm. fees)* houses a trio of museums: The **Asheville Art Museum**★ has bright, airy galleries for displaying regional and modern works; a 376-pound chunk of beryl and a showcase of fluorescent minerals are highlights at the **Colburn' Gem & Mineral Museum**★; and **The Health Adventure** offers exhibits related to human health and science. Behind Pack Place, the **YMI Cultural Center** *(39 S. Market St. 704-252-4614. Tues.-Sat.)* contains African art objects in a wonderful Tudor-style edifice put up by George Vanderbilt for the African-American laborers who helped build his estate.

111

Chimney Rock Park, near Asheville

That residence, **Biltmore Estate** ★★ *(Off US 25. 704-274-6333 or 800-543-2961. Adm. fee)*, is the sole reason many people come to Asheville. A staggering achievement by any measure, the 250-room French Renaissance-style château is especially awesome for a place erected in the 1890s in a remote mountain setting. Vanderbilt had to create a village just to house the stonemasons and artisans that worked on America's largest private house. Its seemingly endless rooms display works of art from throughout the world.

Also seemingly endless, Biltmore's original 125,000 acres allowed Vanderbilt to claim he owned everything he could see, all the way to Mount Pisgah 17 miles in the distance. Still owned by family descendants, the estate now encompasses a modest 8,000 acres.

Take US 74A southeast, following signs for **Chimney Rock Park**★★ *(US 74A. 704- 625-9611. Adm. fee)*, location

Carl Sandburg Home National Historic Site, Flat Rock

for many scenes from the movie *The Last of the Mohicans*. A privately owned attraction since 1902, the stone monolith bursts 315 feet up above the surrounding mountains, providing exquisite views down to Lake Lure. An elevator ascends to the top of the rock, or you can take a series of stairs and boardwalks of heart-racing steepness.

Head southwest on US 64, passing through a land of apple orchards and cornfields, tin-roof shacks and mountain backdrops. Numerous spiritual retreat centers are tucked into the soul-comforting hills of this region.

Take a quick jog on I-26, exiting at Flat Rock for the ❷ **Carl Sandburg Home National Historic Site** *(Off US 25 at 1928 Little River Rd. 704-693-4178. Adm. fee to house)*. In 1945 the 67-year-old poet bought this peaceful 240-acre farm—an ideal place for him to write and for his wife to raise goats. They lived here until his death in 1967. Time has stopped in that year on the Sandburg farm—family furnishings are intact, books are spread on tables, goats browse in the back.

Follow I-26 down to the Tryon exit and pick up US 176, past pottery and weaving shops and a long stretch of crepe myrtles that flower vermilion in summer. At Campobello, turn west on the **Cherokee Foothills Scenic Highway**★ (S.C. 11), and over the next 70 miles be treated to wonderful mountain views, peach orchards, parks, and few other cars; bicyclists seem the only people to have discovered this scenic highway.

The first stop, a 6-mile detour north on Falls Creek Road, **Jones Gap Station** *(864-836-3647)* offers a secluded 3,346 acres in the **Mountain Bridge State**

Natural Area, where you can camp, hike, and fish. Farther along S.C. 11, take the long, twisty climb up US 276 for terrific views of peaks and valleys in **Caesars Head Station★** *(864-836-6115).* From the Visitor Center here, a number of foot trails course out along the rocky ridge.

About 7 miles farther west on S.C. 11, **Table Rock State Park** *(Use west entrance. 864-878-9813. Fee)* has a nature center with native flora and fauna. And the park road offers a great view of the majestic outcrop called Table Rock, but to actually get to it you're in for a long hike. Next stop, **Keowee-Toxaway State Park** *(864-868-2605),* situated on the serene shores of Lake Keowee, harbors good hiking trails and an interpretive center on the Cherokee Indians.

To the northwest, ❸ **Devils Fork State Park** *(Visitor Center 864-944-2639)* nestles in a bowl of mountains along lovely Lake Jocassee, where you can swim or fish. At S.C. 28, turn north and head back toward North Carolina. This slow, curving road, bordered by cool forests, winds up to the state line. Along the way, you cross the wild Chattooga River, popular with white-water runners, and traverse a remote corner of Georgia widely known as *Deliverance* country.

Up above the clouds at over 4,100 feet sits charming **Highlands★,** a leisurely resort town with Main Street sidewalks shaded by colorful shop and restaurant awnings. With a number of historic inns and bed-and-breakfasts, the town is proud of its glorious surroundings. For a fine hike, drive about 6 miles east on US 64 to **Whiteside Mountain★★,** where a 2-mile loop trail follows a high ridge.

The drive continues northwest on US 64. About a mile past Highlands, a turnout beneath a rock overhang lets you drive behind **Bridal Veil Falls.** As you follow **Cullasaja Gorge★** beside its rampant river, look for **Dry Falls★,** where a short trail leads down to a tumultuous curtain of water plunging 75 feet into the gorge.

The next several miles present absolutely gorgeous views of the cliffs, mountains, and more falls of the surrounding Nantahala National Forest *(Highlands Ranger District 704-526-3765).* The gorge levels out, as the Cullasaja slides into the Little Tennessee River near ❹ **Franklin** *(Visitor Center, 425 Porter St. 704-524-3161 or 800-336-7829),* a mining center for gems and minerals. Within a 10-mile radius, more than a dozen mines allow visitors to roll up their sleeves and pan for rubies and sapphires. To know what you're looking for, start with **Ruby City Gems & Minerals★** *(130 E. Main St. 704-524-3967. April- Dec. Mon.-Sat.),* which has a gem shop and a funky museum crammed with treasures and oddities. Equally enlightening

Kudzu Konverts

Not everyone in the South hates kudzu. The broad-leafed green vine covers hillsides, trees, abandoned buildings, and just about anything else that sits still long enough. Imported from Asia in the 1930s to prevent soil erosion, it not only did that but began spreading as much as a foot a day. Some people still try to kill the hardy weed, others just accept it. But a few, such as North Carolina farmers Edith and Henry Edwards of Rutherfordton, turned it to good use. Henry used to bale kudzu for silage and maintains his cows liked it better than corn—and they produced more milk. Edith and other area mavericks are making kudzu jelly, kudzu juice, fried kudzu leaves, kudzu paper, and kudzu-vine baskets and ornaments. The Edwards offer kudzu-wagon rides and kudzu-related activities at Chimney Rock Park. *(For information call the park at 800-277-9611.)*

113

is the **Franklin Gem and Mineral Museum**★ (*25 Phillips St. 704-369-7831. May-Oct. Mon.-Sat.*), which fills the two floors of an 1850 jail with displays of crystals, gems, and Native American artifacts.

From here US 441, an easy four-lane highway, leads up to the mountainside town of **Cherokee** (*Visitor Center, Bus. US 441/19. 704-497-9195 or 800-438-1601*). This is the capital of the eastern band of the Cherokee Indians—descendants of the thousand who eluded the forced march to Oklahoma in 1837-38 along the infamous Trail of Tears. At first glance, the town strip seems to focus on a bingo parlor, a casino, fun parks, and trading posts advertised by wooden bears and live Native Americans in Plains Indian regalia. But behind lurks a number of worthwhile sites.

The town centerpiece, the **Museum of the Cherokee Indian**★ (*US 441N. 704-497-3481. Adm. fee*), is currently undergoing a high-tech renovation and expects to reopen soon. Devoted to 10,000 years of Native American history, the museum explains, among other things, the Trail of Tears tragedy. The dramatic story is retold in an outdoor pageant, ***Unto These Hills*** ★ (*Off US 441N 704-497-2111. Mid-June–Aug. Mon.-Sat.; fee*). Nearby, the **Oconaluftee Indian Village**★ (*704-497-2315. Mid-May–late Oct.; adm. fee*) offers tours of a re-created 1750 Cherokee community, and costumed Native Americans demonstrate such 18th-century skills as canoemaking, finger weaving, and flint chipping.

Now make your way to ❺ **Great Smoky Mountains National Park**★★ (*423-436-1200*). To see how whites hacked a living out of these hills, stop at the **Mountain Farm Museum**★, beside the **Oconaluftee Visitor Center.** Then visit the 520,976-acre park, which encompasses some of the highest and oldest land in the East, as well as an incredible diversity of plant life. Flanking the Cherokee Indian Reservation, the park is a huge drawing card for area tourists. The two-lane main road, an extension of US 441, travels from the Oconaluftee Visitor Center up across the Appalachian Trail and down to Sugarlands Visitor Center on the Tennessee side, about an hour away (see Tennessee Highlands drive, p. 121). The halfway point, 5,048-foot **Newfound Gap** provides spectacular views of peaks and valleys. From here, you can opt to take a 7-mile spur drive to Clingmans Dome (*closed in winter*), at 6,643 feet the park's highest mountain. A half-mile walk to the summit brings you to an observation tower and a cyclorama view of blue mountains.

Turn back to Asheville on the highly scenic **Blue Ridge Parkway**★★ (*704-298-0398*), a ribbon of road that curls and uncurls through tunnels and over ridges, with marvelous

Franklin gems

Along the Blue Ridge Parkway

views and plenty of turnouts. **Waterrock Knob** *(Milepost 451.2)* has information, exhibits, and a trail with vistas of the Smokies. You can end your loop back in Asheville, or continue north along the parkway to the **Folk Art Center**★ *(Mile 382. 704-298-7928)*. This facility presents works for show and sale by members of the Southern Highlands Craft Guild. Artists are on hand to demonstrate cornhusk dollmaking, weaving on old looms, and many other traditional crafts.

Another worthwhile stop, **Craggy Gardens** *(Mile 364.5. Visitor Center May-Oct.)* bursts with rhododendrons in June and with wildflowers throughout the warm months. You're now up above 5,000 feet, where the air is clearer and thinner. Brilliant views will keep your head swiveling as the road swings birdlike over infinite space. Just after Mile 355, turn left and travel 5 miles to the top of ❻ **Mount Mitchell**★★ *(Mount Mitchell State Park. 704-675-4611)*. One of the coldest, windiest places in the South, the 6,684-foot peak ranks as the highest east of the Mississippi. Climb the observation tower beside the 1835 grave of Dr. Elisha Mitchell and drink up the views of blue mountains rolling in timeless ranks to the edge of the sky.

White-tailed deer, Great Smokies

Tennessee Highlands

● **275 miles** ● **3 to 4 days** ● **Year-round** ● **The Smokies are crowded on summer and fall weekends. Do the Cades Cove drive early in the day to avoid crowds.**

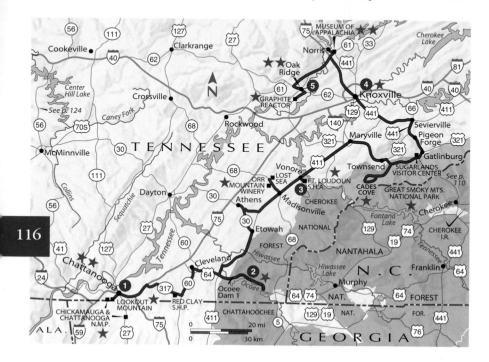

Mountain beauty and city excitement complement each other in the highly popular corridor running between the Tennessee River and the North Carolina border. Varied in scenery and attractions, the drive offers caves, waterfalls, and scenic overlooks, as well as museums, Civil War sites, and historic mansions. Starting in Chattanooga, a tourist destination for more than a century, you'll head northeast, skirt the Cherokee National Forest, and dip down to a river used for white-water events in the 1996 Olympics. Paralleling the mountain ranges to the east as it continues north, the drive stops for Sequoyah's birthplace before making a turn through Great Smoky Mountains National Park. After Dollywood and other country-style fun, you visit Knoxville—a major metropolis in the making—and end at the nearby research city of Oak Ridge, once a government secret.

Built as a riverside trading post, ❶ **Chattanooga**★★ *(Visitor Center, 2 Broad St. 423-266-7070)* became such a strategic rail center that armies of the North and South

smashed into each other here during the
Civil War. After a pivotal victory in the fall of 1863, bored
Yankee soldiers stationed in Chattanooga amused themselves with sight-seeing and picture snapping, becoming
early tourists to the area. They were most impressed with

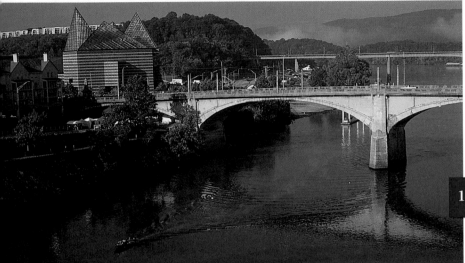

Tennessee Aquarium and Market Street Bridge, Chattanooga

the views from **Lookout Mountain**★, and you can have
the same ones by driving a few miles up a twisty road or
by taking the **Lookout Mountain Incline
Railway**★ *(3917 St. Elmo Ave. 423-821-4224.
Adm. fee)*. In operation since 1895, the railway
inches up a seemingly sheer slope to the top
of the mountain.

For most sites up here you'll need a car.
But from the railway, you can walk over to
Point Park★ *(423-821-7786)*, part of the
**Chickamauga and Chattanooga National Mil-
itary Park**★ *(706-866-9241)*—oldest and
largest military park in the nation. A Visitor
Center holds signalling flags and torches, as
well as the magnificent mural "Battle Above
the Clouds," painted by James Walker just after
the war. Enjoy the splendid views of the city
and of the Tennessee River at Mocassin Bend.

Lookout Mountain Incline Railway

Warhorse of the tourism trade, venerable **Rock City**★
(Lookout Mtn. 706-820-2531. Adm. fee) opened its doors in
1932. Mixing natural beauty with unrestrained kitsch, the
site offers a self-guided tour through narrow defiles,

across a swinging bridge, and out to magnificent over-looks, concluding with a cavern of black-lit tunnels and grottoes lined with elves and other fairyland creatures.

In-town thrills begin with the famous **Chattanooga Choo-Choo** *(1400 Market St., at the Holiday Inn)* that linked northern with southern rail lines. The 1880 engine sits outside a restored railway station that houses shops, restaurants, and a 174-foot-long **Model Railroad** *(423-266-5000 ext. 444. Adm. fee).* A free shuttle runs from the choo-choo down to the **Tennessee Aquarium★** *(1 Broad St. 423-265-0695. Adm. fee),* which protrudes from the water-front in gigantic shards of glass. Inside, a spectacular four-floor presentation of aquatic life includes indoor forests and a 60-foot-deep ocean canyon.

From here you can stroll the riverwalk and the pedestrians-only **Walnut Street Bridge,** a century-old steel-truss span that connects downtown with the shops and restaurants on the north shore. Back on the south side, a zigzagging walkway leads up to the **Bluff View Art District★.** It's worth the climb to this little cliff-top enclave of classy galleries and upscale cafés. The **Hunter Museum of American Art★** *(10 Bluff View. 423-267-0968. Closed Mon.; adm. fee)* has one of the Southeast's preemi-nent collections of American art and choice river views, all in a 1904 neoclassic mansion. Across the lane, the **River Gallery** *(400 E. 2nd St. 423-267-7353)* sells both tradi-tional and outrageous pieces in alabaster, silver, blown glass, baling wire, and oil-on-canvas; the gallery's sculp-ture garden is a hip swirl of plants and artwork.

Head northeast out of town on I-75 to Tenn. 317 and follow signs to **Red Clay State Historical Park** *(Off Tenn. 317, 1140 Red Clay Park Rd. S.W. 423-478-0339),* the site of the Cherokee's last capital before their 1838 removal to Oklahoma. A peaceful place of woods and fields, the park holds the council springs, a reconstructed council house, a 2-mile nature trail, and an Interpretive Center.

Take Tenn. 60 north, then US 64 east to the raging ❷ **Ocoee River★,** venue for the 1996 Olympic white-water canoe- and kayak-slalom races. Though water diver-sion for hydroelectric power kept the Olympic section dry for 40 years, it still ranks as the only natural river to play host to the events. After three years of testing, modeling, and adding boulders and concrete, this section was deemed fit for the big competition. Roadside outfitters offer rafting trips *(June-Aug. Thurs.-Mon., April-May and Sept. Sat.-Sun.)* on a 5-mile stretch of boat-slamming, gut-churning rapids with names like Broken Nose and Doublesuck.

See Rock City

In the annals of advertis-ing, a place of honor surely belongs to Garnet Carter. During the depths of the Great Depression, the cigar-smoking optimist set out to ballyhoo his Lookout Mountain site into a can't-miss attraction. To any farmer who would have "See Rock City" painted on his barn, Carter would throw in a free barn painting to boot. He eventually had to throw in a few dollars and free passes to Rock City as well, but over the years he tallied up 900 barns. And endless streams of visitors. Ladybird Johnson's high-way beautification move-ment in the 1960s spelled the end of such brazen advertising, but about 70 of the original "See Rock City" barns still stand, from Alabama to Ohio.

118

Travel north on US 411, with the high mountains of the Cherokee National Forest to your right. Known as the Overhill, this region was heavily logged and mined for copper in the early part of the century but has since recuperated. Cross the **Hiwassee State Scenic River,** another favorite with white-water fans, and continue north. A diversion west to Athens allows you to take in the **McMinn County Living Heritage Museum** *(522 W. Madison Ave. 423-745-0329. Adm. fee),* a grab bag of Appalachian lore from Cherokee moccasins to Depression-era quilts.

Continue northeast on US 411 to Madisonville and go west on Tenn. 68 a few miles until you see signs for **Orr Mountain Winery**★ *(355 Pumpkin Hollow Rd. 423-442-5340. Closed Mon.-Tues. Sept.-June),* a 10-acre spread that produces 10,000 bottles a year from 5 varieties of grapes. Informative tours follow the grapes from stemmer to press to vat to bottle. Tastings follow. A mile up Tenn. 68, the **Lost Sea** *(423-337-6616. Adm. fee)* features glass-bottom boat rides on a large underground lake; crystal cave flowers and other fantastic formations adorn the surrounding cave walls.

In the 1750s, the British and Cherokee made war against the French. By the end of the decade, though, the British had alienated their Indian allies. Up in Vonore, ❸ **Fort Loudoun State Historic Area**★ *(1 mile off US 411 on Tenn. 360. 423-884-6217)* contains a reconstruction of the garrison the Indians besieged in 1760.

The Cherokee who gave his people the gift of written language was born near the **Sequoyah Birthplace Museum** *(Tenn. 360. 423-884-6246. Adm. fee),* which houses displays on Sequoyah and the Cherokee. For an example of historical ambivalence, compare the Andrew Jackson here—described as an Indian hater who ordered the Cherokee removal to Oklahoma— with the great statesman of The Hermitage (see the Midland Circuit drive, p. 124), who adopted an Indian child.

By Maryville, you'll feel like you're no longer in the mountains, but as you head

Kayaking the Ocoee River

east on US 321 the ranges reappear in ranks. Horse farms shoulder the road here, outlined by plank fences, and houses advertise crafts for sale. West of Townsend, cut through a gap and follow signs to **Tuckaleechee Caverns**

Cades Cove, Great Smoky Mountains National Park

(US 321. 423-448-2274. Mid-March–mid-Nov.; adm. fee). The well-lit cave features waterfalls, jewel-like onyx formations, and stalagmites.

At Townsend, as you enter **Great Smoky Mountains National Park★,** turn right and proceed to **Cades Cove★.** An 11-mile loop road offers a windshield tour of this gorgeous mountain-rimmed vale of meadows and forests. Nearly 700 settlers lived here in the mid-19th century; many log houses, barns, churches, and outbuildings remain. The one-way road tends to fill with traffic in summer, but you can rent a horse or a bike or explore on one of the many hiking trails. The park itself, the most heavily visited of all national parks, often lives up to its name: Fog blankets the valleys and high peaks, and heavy rainfall results in an extravagant variety of plants and flowers. Haze, coupled with air pollution that has cut summertime views by 80 percent in the last 50 years, makes this a park for close-ups rather than panoramas.

From Townsend take the crooked, tree-tunnel Little River Road northeast, spinning along a stream popular for tubing and fishing. Lots of turnouts make it easy to get out and scramble over the rocks to a swimming hole. **Sugarlands Visitor Center** *(US 441. 423-436-1200)* has exhibits, films, and brochures (see The Smokies drive, p. 110).

Spread along the Little Pigeon River, the small resort town of **Gatlinburg** *(Visitors & Convention Bureau*

423-436-2392) crawls with visitors, particularly in summer. Year-round seasonal festivities borrow from the region's highland culture, and there's an extensive crafts community. The **Gatlinburg Aerial Tramway**★ *(1001 Parkway. 423-436-5423. Adm. fee)* makes a vertical ascent of 1,500 feet on a breathtaking 2-mile trip to **Ober Gatlinburg,** an amusement complex with ice skating, winter skiing, and an alpine slide.

Head up US 441 to **Pigeon Forge,** another mountain gateway town. This whole area is booming in popularity, thanks in large part to **Dollywood** *(Off US 441. 423-428-9488. Daily Mem. Day–Labor Day, closed Jan.-March, call for hours rest of year; adm. fee).* The 125-acre theme park has recently passed Opryland as the state's most highly attended private attraction. Rides, music shows, crafts demonstrations, and a museum capitalize on Dolly Parton's homespun charm.

Lower-key attractions in town include the **Historic Old Mill**★ *(2944 Middle Creek Rd. 423-453-4628. Adm. fee),* an operating 1830 gristmill. On tours the miller shows how waterpower turns the grinding stones to produce the corn meal, wheat flour, and grits that are for sale on the premises. Next door, the town's original iron forge once stood. Of the many crafts shops along the street, the 51-year-old **Pigeon Forge Pottery** *(423-453-3883. 2919 Middle Creek Rd.)* lets you walk through the workroom and observe the ceramic-making process.

Continuing north to **Sevierville,** you'll pass lots of newly sprouted venues for country music shindigs and gospel jubilees. There are also several outfits offering helicopter tours of the Smokies. The town's century-old courthouse sports Byzantine domes, a clock tower, and, best of all, a smiling bronze of native Dolly Parton, clutching a guitar and sitting on a boulder.

Welcome to Dollywood

121

State capital until 1812, the glittering Tennessee River city of ❹ **Knoxville**★ boasts a wealth of museums, historic houses, and sleek commercial buildings. It's also home to the University of Tennessee and the Tennessee Valley Authority headquarters. Start out in the Visitor Center *(810 Clinch Ave. 423-523-2316. Closed*

Knoxville's Sunsphere and the Tennessee Amphitheater

Sun.), located at the base of the **Sunsphere.** An unmistakable landmark, the 26-story tower provides good views of the city, river, and distant mountains. The tower presides over what's left of the 1982 World's Fair Park. Though substantially reduced in size since that megafest, the park still has a waterway and greensward and the four-story **Candy Factory,** with its shops, galleries, and arts spaces. New in the park, the **Knoxville Museum of Art** *(1050 World's Fair Park Dr. 423-525-6101. Closed Mon.)* concentrates on contemporary American and touring exhibitions.

Not far away, Knoxville's effort in downtown revitalization has created **Old City**★, a 4-block gaslight district of turn-of-the-century warehouses and office buildings with cupolas, arched windows, and ironwork. Nightclubs, boutiques, and chic restaurants exist within earshot of an active flour factory. The first buildings in town were **James White's Fort**★ *(205 E. Hill Ave. 423-525- 6514. Closed Sun. and mid-Dec.-Feb.; adm. fee)*, a handful of log structures put up in 1786. Relocated to a plot near its original site, the fort's main house now features period furnishings, and costumed guides recall pioneer life. In the late 18th century, the **Blount Mansion**★ *(Gay St. and W. Hill Ave. 423-525- 2375. Closed Mon.; adm. fee)* was considered a model of elegance, but it's now overshadowed by skyscrapers. Built by William Blount, governor of the Southwest Territory, the two-story frame house has a spare formality, brightened by a little garden with river views.

Scoot north on a curvy section of I-75 to Norris, a town created by the Tennessee Valley Authority in the 1930s. Just east, the **Museum of Appalachia**★★ *(Tenn. 61. 423-494-7680. Adm. fee)* embodies the enduring spirit of hardscrabble mountainfolk. More than 30 old buildings have been relocated here from area farms and painstakingly outfitted with authentic household items. Old-timers plant crops, split shingles, can vegetables, and so forth, not just for demonstration, but because it needs doing.

Take Tenn. 61, recently widened to four lanes, southwest to **⑤ Oak Ridge★★,** another new town. This one mushroomed to life in months for the sole purpose of helping produce an atomic bomb during World War II. Tucked away from the eyes of the world, the "secret city" teemed with mechanics and physicists, soldiers and chemists, most of whom did not know what was really going on. They were sworn to secrecy anyway, everyone wore IDs, and armed guards manned security fences. Research continues today on such peaceful projects as nuclear fusion and nuclear-waste disposal.

Begin with the well-stocked **Welcome Center** *(302 S. Tulane Ave. 423-482-7821).* Adjacent is the **American Museum of Science and Energy★** *(300 S. Tulane Ave. 423-576-3200),* which tells the fascinating story of Oak Ridge. In addition to history, the museum lays out the whole energy picture, with lots of neat hands-on stuff upstairs.

To see the cradle of the nuclear age, drive about 10 miles out to the **Graphite Reactor★** *(Bethel Valley Rd. 423-574-4160).* A National Historic Landmark, the world's premier nuclear reactor stands in a tall metal shed amid the crush of Oak Ridge National Laboratory (ORNL) buildings. Exhibits explain how scientists produced plutonium here, unleashing one of the most powerful forces in the universe. You can try out robotic arms in a mock-up "hot cell" and see the reactor's control room.

Just north, an **overlook** offers a good panorama of ORNL; an audiovisual program gives an introduction to the site and explains ongoing research. Nearby, the 1924 **New Bethel Church** *(Bethel Valley Rd.)* is all that remains of the farm communities torn down for Oak Ridge. The little chapel was spared to serve as a meeting room for scientists. Inside are mementoes of the more than 3,000 people forced to give up their homes and leave. Look out one window and see weathered graves from the mid-19th century; from another you can make out the clustered buildings of a new world.

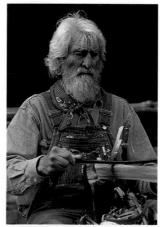

Carver at Museum of Appalachia, Norris

123

● **310 miles** ● **3 days** ● **Year-round**

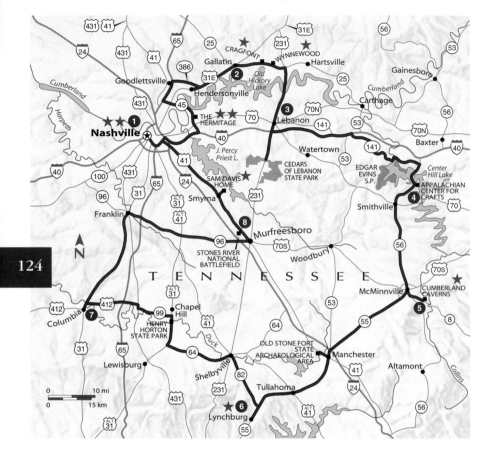

124

Ambling through Tennessee's wide midsection, this drive is a sampler of the upper South's specialties—antebellum homes, Civil War battlefields, whiskey distilleries, country music, and a landscape of rolling foothills, green pastures, lovely lakes, and forests.

The tour begins, and lingers, in Nashville, the state's most exciting city. Fill up on country music, country music museums, country music souvenirs, and—for good measure—a few pre-country music history sites. Then it's off to Andrew Jackson's home and Gallatin's graceful mansions. Crossing the Cumberland River, you'll head south to Lebanon and the avant-garde crafts center tucked into the surrounding hills. As you begin circling clockwise back to Nashville, you explore one of the largest cave rooms in the eastern U.S., the fascinating ruins of a prehistoric

Indian ceremonial complex, and the place where spring water is turned into Jack Daniel's whiskey. The last few towns on the route boast vivid reminders of the Civil War.

Embracing a broad curve of the Cumberland River, the state capital, ❶ **Nashville**★★ *(Convention & Visitors Bureau, 501 Broadway. 615-259-4700)*, started out in 1779

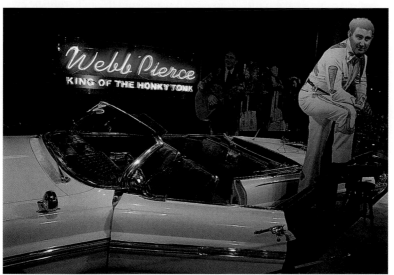

Country Music Hall of Fame and Museum, Nashville

as a pioneer outpost called Fort Nashborough. A century and a half later, a local radio show that aired after a grand opera joked about its home-grown music, calling itself the Grand Ole Opry. From then on, Nashville grew famous as Music City USA.

Begin your tour downtown, an area that arose from the dead a few years ago. The three main drags are **Second Avenue**★, **Printer's Alley**★, and **lower Broadway**★. Ignore the overzealous parking lot attendants as you approach from the south—there are plenty of lots all over the downtown district, closer to where you want to be.

A row of spruced-up Victorian warehouses, Second Avenue teems nightly with tourists. Funky boutiques sell items ranging from pointy boots to hemp shirts. Eating options extend well beyond slouchy coffee shops and popular clones like Hard Rock Cafe. The party-hearty **Wildhorse Saloon** *(120 2nd Ave. N. 615-251-1000)* has a 3,000-square-foot dance floor aswirl with cowboy hats and decorative belt buckles, especially on television taping nights.

Country, western, and blues wail through Printer's Alley,

a short street with a 50-year-old music tradition that has spotlighted Chet Atkins, Waylon Jennings, and Hank Williams. The blinking lights of a strip joint help maintain the unrefined, back-alley atmosphere. Two blocks away, lower Broadway is lined with record stores, guitar shops, and music saloons. The list of country music dignitaries who have started from or at least passed through **Tootsie's Orchid Lounge** ★ *(422 Broadway. 615-726-0463)* runs too long to name, but lots of publicity has done nothing to spoil this tiny, authentic honky-tonk. Signed photos cover cracked walls, and ceiling fans slowly stir the air while the latest crooner entertains tourists, locals, and fellow musicians.

Tootsie's was the traditional watering hole for performers at the **Ryman Auditorium** ★ *(116 5th Ave. N. 615-254-1445. Adm. fee)*, just around the corner. Though dwarfed by the muscular beauties of Nashville's modern skyline, the 105-year-old redbrick Ryman has received the love and attention it deserves as a tabernacle of good music.

You can walk a mile or take a trolley from downtown to **Music Row,** the 10-block nerve center of country music recording since the early 1960s. Souvenir shops, a wax museum, and museums dedicated to individual stars keep sidewalks busy. The **Country Music Hall of Fame and Museum** ★ ★ *(4 Music Sq. E. 615-255-5333. Adm. fee)* offers a crash course in country with exhibits on stars from Hank Williams to Garth Brooks. Movie clips, interactive computers, and hundreds of instruments under glass make this an exciting showcase. Elvis excesses here include his gold-leaf piano and a 1960s Cadillac outfitted with a refrigerator, bar, phonograph, telephone, and gold-plated TV. Tickets include rides on the Nashville trollies for the day, plus

Andrew Jackson's Hermitage, outside Nashville

a narrated Music Row tour and a visit to **RCA Studio B,** the country's second oldest surviving studio (after Sun Studio in Memphis). Such legends as Chet Atkins, Elvis Presley, and Dolly Parton recorded here.

Located 20 minutes by car or 45 minutes by water taxi northeast of downtown, **Opryland USA** ★ *(2808 Opryland*

_Dr. 615-889-6611)_ is a mega entertainment complex that feels as large as an entire city. Within this city, the **Opryland Hotel** is an attraction itself: The massive hotel harbors a 4.5-acre atrium lush with palm trees, a fountain, a 110-foot waterfall, and canals plied by passenger boats.

Outside, you can ride screaming roller-coasters and see music shows at the **Opryland Themepark** _(Adm. fee)_, but you won't see country music stars here unless you hold a ticket for one of the Nashville on Stage performances. But you _will_ see famous singers at the adjacent **Grand Ole Opry★** _(615-889-6611. Shows Fri.-Sat. evenings, Tues. matinees June-Aug.; fee)_. Beside the 4,400-seat house, three museums examine the careers of Roy Acuff, Minnie Pearl, and others.

Now it's time to leave the city and head east on I-40 and north on Tenn. 45 to **The Hermitage★★** _(4580 Rachel's Ln. 615-889-2941. Adm. fee)_, the mansion Andrew Jackson built in 1821, then rebuilt along grander lines after an 1834 fire. A separate museum has personal effects and a film on the seventh President, while the house displays original family furniture. You can wander the extensive grounds past slave cabins and other outbuildings, and watch archaeologists at work during the summer.

Head up Tenn. 45 and avoid traffic by taking I-65 north and the Vietnam Veterans Boulevard (Tenn. 386) to Hendersonville, a community within Nashville's gravitational pull. Take the Saundersville Road exit and go south to **Trinity Music City USA** _(US 31E. 615-826-9191)_ for a free, bizarre tour of the religious broadcasting concern that recently moved here. The tour includes a film and a peek at the house once owned by country musician Conway Twitty.

U.S. Senator Daniel Smith built **Rock Castle** _(S of US 31E on Rock Castle Ln., Hendersonville. 615-824-0502. Feb.-Dec. Wed.-Sun.; adm. fee)_, a limestone house, in 1796 on land granted him for his service in the French and Indian War and his skillful surveying (he made the state's first map). The house has original glass, woodwork, and period furnishings.

Then it's on to **❷ Gallatin** _(Chamber of Commerce, 118 W. Main St. 615-452-4000)_, seat of Sumner County and a center for tobacco, soybeans, and dairying. Two blocks west of the public square stands the 1813 **Trousdale Place** _(183 W. Main St. 615-452-5648. Wed.-Sun.; adm. fee)_. The stalwart brick house of Gov. William Trousdale contains original furniture and a library of Confederate history.

Five miles to the east, **Cragfont★** _(Tenn. 25. 615-452-7070. Mid-April–Oct. Tues.-Sun.; adm. fee)_, still grand by today's standards, must have stunned visitors to the Tennessee wilderness at the turn of the 19th century. That's when Gen. James

Peter Taylor

He grew up in west and middle Tennessee listening to his mother's stories— and paying close attention: "You listen to people talk when you're a child—a Southerner does especially—and they tell stories and stories and stories, and you feel those stories must mean something." To find out what they meant, he began writing stories of his own. And in books like _The Old Forest_ and _A Summons to Memphis_, the Pulitzer Prize winner shined a crystal-clear beam on the southern gentry, and projected the mysteries of the human heart. Although his stories mostly take place between the two World Wars, his characters have a keen sense of the remote past— a sense he knew to be a burden and a blessing, and distinctly southern: "There was the great turning point: Before 1865 is the past; after that, the present. That's dramatic, and it's bound to create stories."

Winchester trekked 600 miles from Maryland with a gang of stonemasons, carpenters, and joiners, and erected his mansion of local limestone, poplar, and walnut. Picture the ballroom bustling with wide skirts and buzzing with the talk of such guests as Andrew Jackson and Sam Houston.

Wynnewood, outside Gallatin

A couple of miles farther on through gentle hills, you come to another fine piece of architecture, this one much less formal. A two-story log inn, the 1828 **Wynnewood**★ *(Tenn. 25. 615-452-5463. Closed Sun. Nov.-March; adm. fee)* served as a stagecoach stop and mineral springs resort. Rocking chairs sit on a wide back porch overlooking the garden. Though the place has a homey charm, modern travelers might object to the communal arrangements—men slept in one room and women in another, on old-fashioned rope beds.

Push south on US 231, past pretty farms with stone outbuildings and plank fences. Recross the wide Cumberland and head for ❸ **Lebanon,** established in 1802 on the stagecoach route and named for its profusion of cedars. The handsome town square sports painted two-story brick buildings, many of them selling antiques and crafts. A landscaped center holds the requisite Confederate veteran's monument, with an added poignancy—a skirmish in 1862 actually swirled through the square, resulting in the burning of many local houses and buildings. A few miles south, you can stretch your legs at the 900-acre **Cedars of Lebanon State Park** *(US 231. 615-443-2769),* an area logged out for its valued cedars (eastern junipers) and replanted by the Civilian Conservation Corps in the 1930s.

Up on I-40, the land grows hillier the farther east you go. About the time you're itching to get out into it, you'll see signs for **Edgar Evins State Park** *(Tenn. 141. 615-858-2446),* a lovely 6,000-acre preserve with a lake nestled in a bowl of hills. Here you can rent cabins or pitch a tent, go for a dip, or cast for bass or walleye.

Hidden away in these hills, the ❹ **Appalachian Center for Crafts** *(Tenn. 56. 615-597-6801)* is the product of a five-million-dollar federal grant, the largest ever to crafts. Full and part-time students work with clay, metal, fiber, wood, and glass, and the results are wonderful—ranging from traditional baskets and quilts to wacky decorative objects.

There are some good lake views as you wend your

way south on Tenn. 56 and down from the hills to a stretch of hayfields and meadows relieved by tangly slopes of kudzu. Drive 7.5 miles southeast of McMinnville to ❺ **Cumberland Caverns** ★ *(Off Tenn. 8; follow signs. 615-668-4396. May-Oct.; adm. fee)*. The cave's 32 miles of passageways make it the state's longest. The 90-minute underground tours pass many gorgeous formations, awe-inspiring when you consider that they grow at the rate of a cubic inch per century. Hanging from the ceiling of one large room, a 1,500-pound chandelier from Loew's Metropolitan Theatre in Brooklyn makes a multicolored spectacle in the cavern gloom. Tours also include a Christian sound-and-light show.

Flat fields edged with wildflowers frame the road as you head southwest to Manchester and the **Old Stone Fort State Archaeological Area** *(N on US 41. 615-723-5073)*. Not a fort in the Daniel Boone sense, these earth and rock walls enclose an area over a mile in circumference that served as a sacred place for Indians of the mid-Woodland Period. The "fort," now a meadow, spreads at the forks of the Duck River, and you can hike wooded trails along the ancient walls and see waterfalls plunging far below. A museum outlines Native American culture, but the fort's full significance remains a mystery.

129

Less mysterious is the appeal of **Jack Daniel's Distillery** ★★ *(Tenn. 55. 615-759-6180)* in ❻ **Lynchburg** ★. The country's oldest registered distillery began operations in 1866 beside a cave spring that Jack Daniel selected for its pure water. Local-born old-timers give free tours that cover the distilling process in detail, including the sweet-smelling room where sour mash whiskey seeps drop by drop through vats of sugar maple charcoal.

Cumberland Caverns

Tours also enter Daniel's original 1860s white-frame office building. Since this is a dry county, you could not buy whiskey here until 1995, when a special act of the state legislature allowed for the sale of a commemorative (expensive) bottle. Or you can have a sample in ice cream or candy down at the village square, a charming quadrangle of antique and gift shops, a general store, a farmer's co-op, and an 1885 barn-red courthouse. For a special treat, reserve a seat for midday dinner at **Miss Mary's Boarding House** *(Main St. 615-759-7394),* a tradition for over 90 years.

Next, head north to Shelbyville on Tenn. 82, a scenic backroad past big meadows and small farmhouses. This is Tennessee Walking Horse country, cradle of the high-stepping, smooth-riding show-offs of the equine world. The Chamber of Commerce *(100 N. Cannon Blvd. 615-684-3482. Mon.-Fri.)* has maps of the nearly 40 area horse farms; call ahead to visit one. The **Tennessee Walking Horse Museum** *(Whitthorne St. 615-684-0314. Mon.-Fri.; adm. fee)* features videos and displays on the current world champion and the history and training of the breed.

Northwest a ways, you come to **Henry Horton State Park** *(Chapel Hill. 615-364-2222),* a 1,200-acre fun zone on the site of an 1800s stagecoach inn and mill. Activities include camping, hiking, golfing, skeet shooting, and swimming.

Continuing west, you enter the Duck River town of **7 Columbia** *(Visitors Bureau, Court House Sq. 615-381-7176),* celebrated for mules and James K. Polk. Columbia has been a mule-trading center for 150 years. The only surviving residence of the 11th President, the **James K. Polk Ancestral Home** *(301 W. 7th St. 615-388-2354. Adm. fee)* was built by his parents in 1816; Polk lived here in his 20s, as he was starting his law practice. Family items and White House gifts abound.

Jack Daniel's Distillery, Lynchburg

The road north unscrolls through a pastoral tableau of rolling countryside, dotted with big spools of hay in summertime and punctuated by old farmhouses and silos. One of the Civil War's ugliest battles occurred in late November 1864 up at **Franklin** *(Williamson County Tourism, City Hall. 615-794-1225).* In the desperate last months of the war, 26,000 Confederates marched across open fields attempting to drive the enemy from Nashville, and they were cut down like blades of summer grass. In five hours of hand-to-hand fighting, 6,000 southern soldiers were lost, including five generals; the Union suffered 2,300 casualties.

Graceful **Carnton Plantation**★ *(1345 Carnton Ln. 615-794-0903. Adm. fee),* though encroached on by a new housing development, still has enough surrounding fields to put you in the past. The house became a hospital for hundreds of wounded men after the 1864 battle—heavy bloodstains on the floors attest to the carnage. From the back second-

Stones River National Battlefield, Murfreesboro

story veranda, you can look out to the McGavock Confederate Cemetery holding some 1,500 graves.

While family members hid in the cellar, a hailstorm of minié balls whistled around the 1830s **Carter House** *(1140 Columbia Ave. 615-791-1861. Adm. fee),* whose outbuildings are still riddled with bullet holes. A visitor center has a video and museum.

Travel east on Tenn. 96 to **Murfreesboro** *(Chamber of Commerce, 302 S. Front St. 615-893-6565),* the state capital from 1819 to 1825. A 26-foot stone obelisk, a mile from downtown, marks the geographical center of Tennessee. Now a trafficky university town, Murfreesboro was a railroad supply line during the Civil War. A few months after Confederate Gen. Nathan Bedford Forrest's successful raid in July 1862, a major three-day battle took place here and the town reverted to Union hands. ❽ **Stones River National Battlefield** *(Off US 41. 615-893-9501)* memorializes the brutal conflict that engulfed 80,000 men. A 5-mile auto tour passes such points as the "slaughter pen," where according to a Union officer, "the dead and wounded lay in heaps."

Another token of those tragic times stands about 12 miles north in Smyrna. Down a long driveway bordered by cedars and groomed fields, the 1820 **Sam Davis Home**★ *(1399 Sam Davis Rd. 615-459-2341. Adm. fee)* was the residence of a 21-year-old Confederate captured about 60 miles from home and, for refusing to betray his fellow soldiers, was hung.

Heading north, pop some Hank Williams into the tape deck and ease back into Nashville.

West Tennessee Loop

● **335 miles** ● **2 days** ● **Year-round**

This relaxing drive through Tennessee's flatlands takes off from the state's largest city then meanders across an agricultural region known for cotton, corn, soybeans, and small towns.

Beginning in Memphis, you get a good taste of the colorful roots of pop music and brush against history from the Civil War to civil rights. Moving into an unspectacular but friendly area of the state, you'll find a few surprises—Indian mounds from the time of Christ, the humble home of a Pulitzer Prize winner, and a ferry operating on the Tennessee River.

Beale Street, Memphis

Perched on a bluff of the Mississippi, ❶ **Memphis**★★ *(Visitors Information Center, 340 Beale St. 901-543-5333 or 800-873-6282)* is a smooth blend of southern aristocracy and jaunty nightlife. Take, for example, downtown. The big, no-nonsense buildings on Front Street, featured in *The Firm* and other movies, are the business end of Memphis—the country's largest inland cotton market since 1870. **Confederate Park** *(Front St. and Madison Ave.)* honors the Southern Cause, lost here in 1862 when Union gunboats made quick work of local defenses.

Five blocks away, the riffs and howls of blues spill from open doorways on **Beale Street**★★. The place where many tourists start and end their touring, the street is a far cry from its rough-edged days as a strip of all-night honky-tonks, gambling dens, and cathouses. W.C. Handy composed "Memphis Blues" here in 1909, the height of the rollicking good times. Almost bulldozed in the 1970s, Beale Street was revived, and today has both the protective coating of a historic attraction and the edgy buzz of creative possibility. Clubs like **B.B. King's**★ *(143 Beale St. 901-524-5464 or 800-334-8959)* feature the best blues musicians around. A fun joint for beer and barbecue is **Beale St. Bar-B-Que** *(205 Beale St. 901-526-6113. Wed.-Sun.),* a

Memphis skyline

homegrown restaurant and piano bar walled with celebrity photos; ask the owner for the stories behind them.

To find out how black blues combined with white country music to create rock and roll, drive over to **Sun Studio**★ *(706 Union Ave. 901-521-0664 or 800-441-6249. Adm. fee),* the redbrick recording facility where the likes of Elvis Presley, Jerry Lee Lewis, B.B. King, and Roy Orbison got their starts. Ringo Starr, U2, and Tom Petty have made recordings here in recent years.

The **National Civil Rights Museum**★★ *(Lorraine Motel, 450 Mulberry St. 901-521-9699. Wed.-Mon.; adm. fee)* offers an emotional careen through the turbulent 1950s and '60s with full-size bus and lunch-counter exhibits. The facade of the motel where Martin Luther King, Jr., was shot remains a shrine to the Nobel Prize-winning leader.

Back up Union Street, the **Memphis Music Hall of Fame Museum**★ *(97 S. 2nd St. 901-525-4007. Adm. fee)* houses an excellent collection of recordings, videos, and memorabilia. Highlights include a Jerry Lee Lewis piano, a

Johnny Cash guitar, a display on bluesman Robert Johnson, and a vivid mural of P. Wee's Saloon during the rowdy days of Beale Street.

Other fine museums are spread all over town. **Mud Island** *(125 N. Front St. 901-576-7241. Closed Mon. Labor Day–Mem. Day; adm. fee),* an extensive riverside park, offers a museum, a tremendous swimming pool, and a 5-block-long scale model of the lower Mississippi.

134

Elvis Presley's Graceland, Memphis

Opened in 1996, the **Hunt-Phelan Home** *(533 Beale St. 901-525-8225. Closed Tues.-Wed. Sept.-March; adm. fee),* one of the oldest houses in the city, was completed in 1832. A Beale Street anachronism, this robust mansion has hosted Jefferson Davis, Andrew Jackson, Nathan Bedford Forrest, and Ulysses S. Grant.

The **Memphis Brooks Museum of Art** *(Overton Park. 901-722-3500. Closed Mon.)* holds a fine survey of world art, including baroque and Impressionist paintings, American portraits, and some wonderful African masks from the late 19th century. A more specialized and intimate museum, the **Dixon Gallery and Gardens**★ *(4339 Park Ave. 901-761-2409. Gallery closed Mon.; adm. fee)* is a lovely oasis concocted by a philanthropic couple. Their house contains works by Gauguin, Degas, Reynolds, Cassatt, and Matisse.

For many people, Memphis means only one thing. But whether or not you're an ardent fan of Elvis Presley, it would be a shame to miss **Graceland**★ *(3734 Elvis Presley Blvd. 901-332-3322 or 800-238-2000. Mansion closed Tues. Nov.-Feb.; adm. fee).* At age 22, Elvis bought the 1939 neoclassic mansion for $100,000 cash. He died here in 1977. The house is a poor country boy's unbridled dream of success—a white, 15-foot custom sofa reigns over the living room; a mirrored staircase leads to a pool room; and a jungle den features wall carpet and a waterfall.

Leaving the only major city within a 150-mile radius, head east on US 64 through a sea of beans, corn, cotton, and tobacco. Just before Whiteville, stop at **Backermann's Bakery** *(US 64. 901-254-8473)* for delicious homebaked goodies and cheeses. Continue to ❷ **Bolivar,** a county seat burned by Union troops during the Civil War. Surviving buildings include the 1824 **Little Courthouse** *(116 E. Market St.)*, a two-story white clapboard that served as the courthouse before the 1868 brick one was built.

Keep bearing east until you come to **Adamsville.** Here you'll learn of the short life of Buford Pusser, the McNairy County sheriff portrayed in the *Walking Tall* movies. In the 1950s and '60s, the Mississippi state line, a few miles south, was a free-for-all of bootlegging, gambling, and prostitution. The six-foot-six lawman went about shutting the party down, an unpopular move that led to the murder of his wife. The **Buford Pusser Home and Museum**★ *(342 Pusser St. 901-632-1401. Adm. fee)*, a simple ranch-style house, contains memorabilia and a film interview of Pusser's daughter.

Large-scale violence occurred south of here in April 1862. ❸ **Shiloh National Military Park**★★ *(Tenn. 22. 901-689-5696. Adm. fee)* preserves the site where 3,500 men died and 16,500 were wounded fighting for control of a railroad. The two-day battle for the vital link between Memphis and Richmond ended in a Union victory, opening the way to Vicksburg and control of the Mississippi. The Visitor Center has a few artifacts and a film. A 10-mile auto tour covers the serene meadows and woods that rang with cannon fire and the cries of the dying.

Travel south on Tenn. 142, then east to Tenn. 57 and the Tennessee River. The **Pickwick Landing Dam** *(Tenn. 57 and Tenn. 128)* operates a fine Visitor Center with exhibits on the TVA Waterway. Fans of mammoth engineering projects can walk out on the walls of the 1,000-foot-long chamber and view the dam's tremendous spillways.

In March 1862, just before the Battle of Shiloh, William T. Sherman's troops occupied tiny **Savannah.** The **Tennessee River Museum** *(507 Main St. 901-925-2364 or 800-552-3866. Adm. fee)* harbors a good collection of area artifacts, including trilobites, projectile points, Civil War gunboat relics, and a prehistoric effigy pipe. The Visitor Center is located here, too.

Now go east a few blocks on US 64 and turn north, rejoining Tenn. 128. You'll pass Cerro Gordo, distinguished only by a two-story general store on the riverbank, and about 4 miles later there's a sign for a ferry. Fork left on Russell Chapel Lane, then in about half a mile turn left on Wilkinson Ferry Drive (if you pass a white chapel, you've gone too far). The road arrows

State Song

In March of 1947 Redd Stewart and Pee Wee King were traveling from a performance, their truck radio tuned to the Grand Ole Opry. Pee Wee asked Redd why he'd never written a song about his home state. So right there, Redd began scribbling on a matchbox the words to the "Tennessee Waltz." A veteran songwriter, he offered this new one to a young singer for $25. He was turned down, and the tune sat in his guitar case for several years. Then in 1950 a rising star named Patti Page needed one more song for a recording session. Released in May, the song sold some five million copies by November, and became one of the country's most popular songs.

through wide fields of soybeans as it makes its way to the river. You'll think you're at the end of the earth, until you come upon a smattering of houses on stilts, graced by motorboats and satellite dishes.

Soon to be the last on the Tennessee, the **Saltillo Ferry** *(901-925-4993. Mon-Sat.; fare)* has operated since 1825. The barge takes only minutes to pull the four-car ferry across the river; honk to hail it from the other side.

Continue northwest toward Pinson on Tenn. 69, Tenn. 22, Tenn. 100, and US 45. The ❹ **Pinson Mounds State Archaeological Area**★ *(2.5 miles E of US 45, 460 Ozier Rd. 901-988-5614. Closed Sat.-Sun. Dec.-Feb.)* contains a dozen earth mounds constructed by Woodland Indians between 200 B.C. and A.D. 50. At 72 feet, one of them ranks as the second highest in the country. Built for ceremonies long before the arrival of Europeans, the tremendous mounds give perspective to the long march of humanity in this quiet neck of the woods. In the side of one mound, the Visitor Center displays stone tools and pendants, and engraved rattles made of human skulls.

Shiloh National Military Park

Continue north on US 45 to **Jackson** *(Convention & Visitors Bureau 901-425-8333)*. Settled in 1819, the town became a rail center and cotton depot, then a Union supply base. Now a busy interstate town of colleges, industries, and agricultural concerns, Jackson boasts several fancy Victorian houses on East Main Street.

The popular **Casey Jones Home and Railroad Museum** *(Casey Jones Village, I-40 and US 45 Bypass. 901-668-1222. Adm. fee)* tells the story of the legendary engineer who crashed his way into immortality on April 30, 1900. The resulting ballad, which sold millions of copies, was penned by engine wiper Wallace Sanders, whose only payment was supposedly a pint of gin. Jones's white clapboard home is filled with early railroading memorabilia. Outside stands a replica of his locomotive; a separate building holds model trains that operate for a quarter.

Along the Hatchie River a few miles south of I-40, the 11,556-acre ❺ **Hatchie National Wildlife Refuge** *(Tenn. 76. 901-772-0501)* is a stop for some 25,000 ducks during their annual migrations and some 200 species of birds.

Take Tenn. 19 north to **Brownsville** *(Chamber of Commerce 901-772-2193)*, settled by Col. Richard Nixon in 1821. A pleasant fountain and shade trees adorn a somewhat down-in-the-mouth courthouse square. The Civil War monument here judiciously honors Confederate *and* Union veterans. The 1851 **College Hill Center** *(129 N. Grand Ave. 901-772-4883. Closed Wed. and Fri.-Sun.)* houses a collection of Haywood County artifacts, as well as Abraham Lincoln memorabilia.

Alex Haley House Museum

Continue northwest on Tenn. 19 and make your way west, slowing for the eye-blink town of Nutbush, birthplace of Tina Turner. The best time for traveling in this direction is morning, when the long shadows catch the farmlands and little churches at their best.

In one of these small towns, a young boy listened to the stories of his grandmother and his aunts, and when he grew up he turned them into a book called *Roots.* In **Henning,** you'll pass some grinding poverty—houses with caved-in roofs and peeling paint—which makes it seem all the more remarkable that a Pulitzer Prize winner was nurtured in the area. The **Alex Haley House Museum** ★ *(200 S. Church St. 901-738-2240. Closed Mon.; adm. fee),* one of the nicer homes in the neighborhood, is the 1919 bungalow built by Haley's grandfather, a successful businessman. Alex lived here for the first eight years of his life and spent many subsequent summers with his grandparents. The house displays his writings and his personal effects.

An ironic counterpoint to the Haley site, ❻ **Fort Pillow State Historic Area** *(18 miles W of Henning via Tenn. 87 and Tenn. 207. 901-738-5581)* is a long but worthwhile side excursion. It preserves the site of one of the Civil War's most controversial battles. In April of 1864, Nathan Bedford Forrest led 1,500 Confederates against 500 untested Union soldiers, most of them black. The fort's defenders refused to surrender and taunted Forrest's men. Enraged, the southern contingent went on a killing spree. Forrest had to ride in front of his men, waving his pistol to stop their massacre, but by then most of the northern opposition had been killed. "The slaughter was awful," wrote one Confederate soldier. Trails lead to Union breastworks, and an Interpretive Center has a film and displays.

Head back to Memphis on US 51.

Land Between the Lakes

● **290 miles** ● **2 days** ● **Spring through fall**

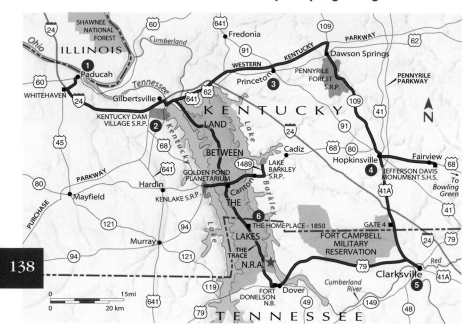

Rural landscapes and a pristine wilderness area surround you on this scenic turn through western Kentucky. With both natural history and cultural attractions, about the only thing this drive lacks is a big-city buzz. Embarking from the riverboat town of Paducah, the route swings

At the Museum of the American Quilter's Society

east across two tremendous Tennessee Valley Authority dams, then pauses in tiny Princeton for an unusually inventive living history museum. It pivots south along hay meadows, cornfields, and small towns on a pilgrimage to the Confederate President's birthplace. Dipping into Tennessee, the drive takes in a military reservation, an industrial town, and an important Civil War battlefield before finishing with a leisurely northward cruise up a long tongue of land between two giant lakes, featuring herds of bison and elk, a 19th-century farmstead, and jewel-like state parks.

Built at the confluence of the Tennessee and Ohio Rivers, ❶ **Paducah** was platted in 1827 by Gen. William Clark, who acquired the 37,000-acre tract of land from the estate of his also famous brother George Rogers Clark for five dollars. A good buy, since the site's riverside location makes it a natural shipping point for commodities such as tobacco and lumber and a port of call for tourists from the *Mississippi Queen* and other riverboats.

The first stop in Paducah is **Whitehaven** *(I-24 and US 45. 502-554-2077)*, a gracious 1860s house converted in 1903 to a classical revival mansion. Wonderful before-and-after photos show what a wreck this fine place, with its curved portico and Corinthian columns, was prior to its 1980s restoration. You can tour the house, which now serves as a state Welcome Center. Pick up walking tour maps here or at the Visitors Bureau *(128 Broadway. 502-443-8783 or 800-723-8224)*.

One of the many historical markers downtown says that Ulysses S. Grant arrived in 1861, leaving Paducah in Union hands for the rest of the war. But the military presence was not enough to prevent Confederate leader Nathan Bedford Forrest from destroying many Lower Town houses. After the war, new houses arose in the Italianate and Queen Anne styles with turrets, balconies, and stained glass. Downtown itself holds a num-

Downtown Paducah

ber of Victorian and classical revival buildings, as well as a pleasant waterfront area where you can get a sandwich, stroll brick sidewalks down to the riverwalk, and watch children dipping their feet and barges plying the Ohio. On the flood wall, itinerant artists are creating a series of colorful murals of early Paducah.

The 1905 **Market House** has an **Art Center** *(200 Broadway. 502-442-2453. Feb.-Dec. Tues.-Sun.; adm. fee)* displaying regional and international arts, and a **museum** *(502-443-7759. March-Dec. Tues.-Sun., Jan.-Feb. weekends only; adm. fee)* full of curiosities, including a life-size statue of Henry Clay carved by a 12-year-old.

A couple of blocks away, the one-of-a-kind **Museum of the American Quilter's Society** *(215 Jefferson St. 502-442-8856. April-Oct. Tues.-Sun., Nov.- March Tues.-Sat.; adm. fee)* pays homage to contemporary quilters. The 30,000-square-foot, climate-controlled facility allows ample room for the display of 150 quilts ranging in design from traditional patterns to brilliant sunbursts to three-dimensional graphics.

Take I-24 east toward Gilbertsville, near the northwest corner of the Land Between the Lakes, and stop at ❷ **Kentucky Dam Village State Resort Park** *(US 641 and US 62. 502-362-4271)* for a refreshing dip in Kentucky Lake and perhaps a round of golf. You can also rent boats, play tennis, and fish.

After you cross the mighty Kentucky Dam, pull into the parking lot at the **Kentucky Dam Lock and Powerhouse** *(US 62. 502-362-4318)* for a closer look at the dam that created the lake and, with Lake Barkley, the Land Between the Lakes. The 53-year-old Kentucky Dam is the longest in the Tennessee Valley Authority system; the resulting Kentucky Lake, occupying 2,380 miles of shoreline, is TVA's largest reservoir. The project claims at least one unfortunate superlative—the highest number of families displaced by the TVA, more than 2,600. Built mostly for flood control and navigation, the dam also generates electricity, as you can see when you duck into the turbine room and view the surprisingly undeafening five great turbine generators. Outside, watch big barges laden with coal, salt, limestone, and grain lock through the channel.

Save the Land Between the Lakes for the end of the trip and continue east to ❸ **Princeton** *(Chamber of Commerce 502-365-5393)*, a small town with a high density of noteworthy architecture, ranging from the 1940 art deco **Caldwell County Courthouse** to the circa 1817 federal **Champion-Sheperdson House** *(115 E. Main St. 502-365-3959. March-Dec. Tues.-Sat.)*. Now the home of the Princeton Art Guild, it exhibits local and imported works. You

View from Jefferson Davis Monument, Fairview

140

can buy prize winning hams, lye soap, homemade jams, and fresh local produce at **Newsom's Old Mill Store** *(208 E. Main St. 502-365-2482. Mon.-Sat.)*, an authentic country market established in 1917 on the site of an 1870 mill.

The reason most people stop in Princeton, though, is for **Adsmore**★ *(304 N. Jefferson St. 502-365-3114. Adm. fee)*, an 1857 mansion operating now as a living history museum. Depending upon the time of year, guests may find the house decorated for a Victorian wedding, a wake, a Christmas celebration, or one of five other themes. Original family documents, furniture, and heirlooms lend realism to the experience.

Now head east on the Western Kentucky Parkway and then south on Ky. 109 to **Dawson Springs,** at one time a thriving mineral springs resort and now an unpretentious little town.

Continue south on Ky. 109, threading dense woods relieved by small farms with weathered old barns and rusty sheds of the kind favored by photographers of the rural South. Along here, houses with vine-covered fences advertise woodcarving, pottery, and other crafts for sale.

❹ **Hopkinsville** *(Chamber of Commerce 502-885-9096 or 800-842-9959)*, seat of Christian County and the heart of dark-fire (fire-cured) tobacco country, is a festival-loving town, holding about a dozen throughout the year. It also sports the worthy **Pennyroyal Area Museum** *(217 E. 9th St. 502-887-4270. Mon.-Sat.; adm. fee)* with exhibits on the Civil War, Trail of Tears, Night Riders of the 1904 tobacco wars, and locally born clairvoyant Edgar Cayce; walking tour brochures are also available here.

Next, take a 10-mile detour east on US 68 to the **Jefferson Davis Monument State Historic Site** *(US 68, Fairview. 502-886-1765. May-Oct.; adm. fee)*. The Washington Monument-like obelisk honoring the Confederacy's first and only President rises out of the surrounding farmland like a totem, reflecting the area's southern heritage. Jefferson Davis was born in Fairview in 1808, less than a year before and a hundred miles from where Abraham Lincoln was born. The 351-foot monument has an elevator up to a panorama of the countryside.

Now double back to Hopkinsville along billowing fields of fescue, clover, and orchard grass, and travel south on US 41A to Fort Campbell Military Reservation. You'll have to show various documents and sign your name a few times to get in (at Gate 4), but in a few minutes you'll arrive at the **Don F. Pratt Museum** *(502-798-3215)*, chronicling the 101st Airborne Division, the "Screaming Eagles." Here you can see uniforms, aircrafts, photographs, and weapons.

Beachaven wines, Clarksville

Then head on to **5** **Clarksville** *(Tourist Commission, 180 Holiday Rd. 615-647-2331 or 800-530-2487)*, sprawled at the confluence of the Cumberland and Red Rivers. Situated within the historical downtown architectural district, the **Clarksville-Montgomery County Museum** *(200 S. 2nd St. 615-648-5780. Closed Mon.; adm. fee)* is an eye-catching potpourri of Renaissance Revival, Romanesque, and Gothic styles with a pyramid roof, dormer windows, tower, and cupola. Originally the post office, the museum houses exhibits on regional history, including a nice collection of horse-drawn vehicles.

Overlooking the Cumberland River, the dignified **Smith/Trahern Mansion** *(1st and McClure Sts. 615-648-9998. Mon.-Fri.; adm. fee)* was built in 1859 with tobacco money. The Greek Revival and Italianate house features jib windows, a curved staircase, and a widow's walk.

Before leaving the area, stop at the **Beachaven Winery** *(E of I-24 at 1100 Dunlap Ln. 615-645-8867)*, where you can learn about the harvesting, pressing, fermenting, and bottling of grapes. Free tours and tastings are offered.

Back on the highway, take US 79 west to **Fort Donelson National Battlefield** *(Dover. 615-232-5706)*, scene of the North's first major victory in the Civil War on Feb. 12-15, 1862. Under the leadership of an obscure brigadier general named Ulysses S. Grant, Union forces won the battle and 13,000 Southern prisoners. Grant's famous ultimatum called for "an unconditional and immediate surrender." The Visitor Center has artifacts and a video; a 6-mile drive courses out to a fine river view from the Confederate batteries.

Now it's time to enter the **Land Between the Lakes National Recreation Area**★ *(502-924-2000 or 800-525-7077)*, the 40-mile-long spit of land between Kentucky and Barkley Lakes, created by the damming of the Tennessee and Cumberland Rivers. The 170,000-acre recreation area is cut by the Trace, a gorgeous stretch of road with Visitor Centers at its south, middle, and north ends. Stop in at one for information on the 200 miles of hiking and biking trails over the area's gentle hills, as well as details on wildlife viewing, camping, hiking, and boating.

Inviting wildflower meadows and tall, feathery grasses disappear into the treeline as you head north on the Trace. After a few miles, use the pull-off on the left to view the resident herd of bison grazing in a 200-acre pasture. The herd started with 19 animals transplanted from North Dakota and now numbers 60 to 70.

Across the highway, **6** **The Homeplace—1850** *(502-924-2000. March-Nov.; adm. fee)* is a living history farm

Corvettes Only

Just off I-65 in Bowling Green, an 11-story red spire projects through a volcano-shaped yellow building, whose parking lot has special spaces for Corvettes only. Welcome to the **National Corvette Museum** *(502-745-8419. Mon.-Fri.)*, the world's largest museum dedicated to one kind of car. Opened in 1994, the sleek 15-million-dollar showcase teaches that it's okay to love a classy sports car. Full-size dioramas spotlight the Vette in such nostalgic scenes as a 1950s barbershop, a 1960s service station, and a Route 66 road trip; films and exhibits look at racing, performance, and crash testing. At the assembly plant across the street, watch Corvettes being made— at the approximate rate of 15 an hour.

Along the Trace, Land Between the Lakes National Recreation Area

with costumed interpreters engaged in farm chores. Nestled in here so far from any urban noise, the place has an eerily authentic feel—as though you, in your tourist clothes, were an alien from the future rather than a visitor to the past. A breezy porch here, a bleating ewe there, the sounds of birds and hammering, and the mingled fragrance of woodsmoke, horses, and curing tobacco make you want to pick up an ax and split some rails.

You can escape back to the future at the **Golden Pond Planetarium** *(502-924-2000. March-Nov.; adm. fee),* where multimedia effects are projected onto a 40-foot dome.

The Homeplace—1850

Drive a few miles west on US 68, across Kentucky Lake, to family-oriented **Kenlake State Resort Park** *(US 68 and Ky 94. 502-474-2211 or 800-323-0143)* for nine holes of golf, a game of tennis, or a swim in the lake (or pool if you're an overnight guest). Or try the **Lake Barkley State Resort Park** *(E of the Trace, off US 68 near Canton. 502-924-1131. Fee for some activities),* which has an 18-hole golf course, a trap range, accommodations both rustic and luxurious, horseback riding, hiking, a beach, and a marina.

Back on the Trace, go a mile north to the **Elk and Bison Prairie** *(Adm. fee),* a 750-acre preserve with a 3.5-mile loop drive for spotting the shaggy beasts once common in these parts. Follow the Trace north to US 62 to complete the drive.

Bluegrass-Cave Country★

● 345 miles ● 2 to 3 days ● Year-round ● Advance reservations required for longer tours of Mammoth Cave ● Book lodging and tickets for the Kentucky Derby, held the first Saturday in May, a year ahead.

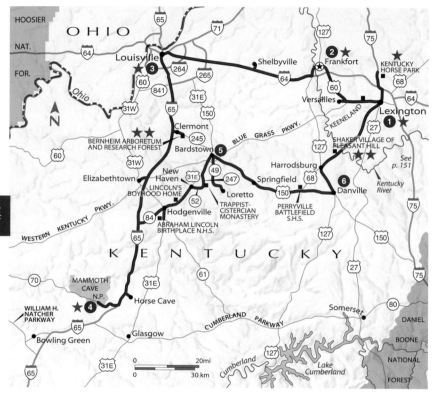

Looping through the rolling hills of central Kentucky, this pastoral drive takes in most of the highlights of the state. The route begins in the lush green horse country around Lexington, then shoots west through the state capital of Frankfort and on to lively Louisville, home of the Kentucky Derby. Turning south, it takes in Mammoth Cave National Park, the world's longest known cavern system, then heads north to Lincoln country and a stop at My Old Kentucky Home. On the way back to Lexington, tour a famous whiskey distillery, a Trappist-Cistercian monastery, a Civil War battlefield, a pioneer fort, and a Shaker village.

Almost from the start, ❶ **Lexington**★ *(Visitor Center, 301 E. Vine St. 606-233-1221 or 800-845-3959)* hitched its wagon to the horse. With gentleman farmers racing Virginia Thoroughbreds through the town streets in the

1780s, Lexington's equine industry was off and running. Now a preeminent center of horse breeding, the area boasts over 500 horse farms that gentle the landscape into a serenade of green, accented by hundreds of miles of white and black plank fences.

Begin with a visit to **Kentucky Horse Park**★ *(I-75 and Iron Works Pike. 606-233-4303. Closed Mon.-Tues. Nov.-March; adm. fee),* over 1,000 acres of horse things for aficionados as well as the merely curious. You can watch movies, see horse shows, take carriage and pony rides, view more than 40 breeds, visit the outstanding International Museum of the Horse, and pay your respects to Man o' War, buried beneath a colossal bronze likeness.

While in the area, meander the narrow, twisty backroads past some exquisite horse farms, announced by imposing stone pillars and iron gates.

In town, historic houses include elegant **Ashland, The Henry Clay Estate**★ *(120 Sycamore Rd. 606-266-8581. Feb.-Dec. Tues.-Sun.; adm.*

fee), home of statesman Henry Clay; and the Georgian **Mary Todd Lincoln House**★ *(578 W. Main St. 606-233-9999. March-Nov. Tues.-Sat.; adm. fee),* where Lincoln's wife spent part of her girlhood.

Arrive before 10 a.m. at **Keeneland** *(W on US 60. 606-254-3412. Adm. fee to races)* and watch horses churning the sand on their morning workouts *(mid-*

Kentucky Horse Park, Lexington

March–early Nov.). At the track kitchen, have breakfast in the company of trainers and, occasionally, jockeys.

Follow US 60 west to **Versailles** *(Chamber of Commerce 606-873-5122),* which preserves a number of antebellum and Victorian buildings. The modest 1797 **Jack Jouett House** *(255 Craig Creek Rd. 606-873-7902. April-Oct. Wed., Sat.-Sun.; donation)* was the home of a Patriot hero and early horse importer, and the **Woodford County Historical Society Museum** *(121 Rose Hill. 606-873-6786. Tues.-Sat.)* contains

Belle of Louisville

Day at the Races

Long shot, chalk horse, breaking maiden, post parade—all part of the lingo of horse racing, the state's favorite sport. If wagering on a trifecta or an exacta intimidates you, if you're even loathe to put good money on an odds-on favorite, don't worry. Racetracks are eager to educate you in the fundamentals of betting and to supply you with course conditions, race records, medication stats, and dozens of other pieces of arcana. Or you can skip the education and simply walk up to the betting window and say, "Five dollars to show on Number Seven." If your horse finishes in the top three, you make money.

exhibits housed in an 1819 federal-style brick building.

Then on to hilly, scenic ❷ **Frankfort**★ *(Visitor Center, 100 Capital Ave. 502-875-8687)*, state capital for more than two centuries. Situated on curves in the Kentucky River, this town-size city boasts an attractive skyline of spires and cupolas and a downtown walking mall. For a bluff-top view of river and town, stop by Daniel and Rebecca Boone's alleged grave in the **Frankfort Cemetery**★ *(215 E. Main St. 502-227-2403)*—marble reliefs depict the pioneer in heroic scenes; his wife is shown milking a cow.

The **Old State Capitol**★ *(Broadway and Lewis St. 502-564-3016)*, the only pro-Union state capitol occupied by the Confederate Army, is a splendid Greek Revival structure with freestanding spiral staircases made of limestone. On the way down to the new capitol, drop by **Rebecca-Ruth Candies** *(112 E. 2nd St. 502-223-7475 or 800-444-3766. Tours Mon.-Sat.)* for a tour of the bourbon chocolate factory started by two sisters during Prohibition. The impressive 1910 beaux arts **Kentucky State Capitol**★ *(700 Capitol Ave. 502-564-3449)* has lots of grand stairways, august statuary, and echoing corridors.

Follow I-64 west across long sweeps of green pasture dotted with trees and hillocks. If you like to antique, detour a little north on Ky. 55 to **Shelbyville.** Back on I-64, you'll round a bend and suddenly see the bridges and skyscrapers of ❸ **Louisville**★ *(Visitor Center, 400 S. 1st St. 502-582-3732)*, the Ohio River city with southern charm and northern energy. The 4-mile **Riverwalk** gives good views of the Falls of the Ohio and a historic dockside neighborhood. From here the 1914 ***Belle of Louisville*** *(401 W. River Rd. 502-574-2992. Mem. Day–Labor Day Tues.-Sun.; fee)* takes passengers on steamboat excursions.

Among downtown architecture, top honors go to the

imposing 1837 Greek Revival **Jefferson County Court-house** *(5th and W. Jefferson Sts.)* and the 1852 **Cathedral of the Assumption** *(443 S. 5th St. 502-583-3100),* with its wonderful deep blue vaulted ceiling. Also, don't miss the 120-foot baseball bat outside **Hillerich & Bradsby** *(800 W. Main St. 502-588-7227. Adm. fee),* a bat factory and museum. The **Louisville Science Center** *(727 W. Main St. 502-561-6100. Adm. fee),* housed in restored 19th-century buildings, harbors three floors of exhibits, including a space-science gallery, an Egyptian mummy, and an IMAX theater.

Drive down Third Street for an eyeful of Victorian mansions built with tobacco and railroad money—some now B&Bs. The **J.B. Speed Art Museum** *(2035 S. 3rd St. 502-636-2893. Closed until late 1997)* holds works by Rembrandt, Monet, Rodin, Picasso, and other greats.

The state's most famous event takes place every year at **Churchill Downs** *(700 Central Ave. 502-636-4400. Adm. fee for races).* A tradition since 1875, the Kentucky Derby, or Run for the Roses, is known as the greatest two minutes in sports. The 360-degree multimedia show at the **Kentucky Derby Museum**★★ *(704 Central Ave. 502-637-7097. Adm. fee)* re-creates the thrill of the derby; exhibits on jockeys, famous horses, and betting reaffirm the region's obsession with horse racing. Afterward, tour the track and grandstand area, where a million dollars is wagered on a good day.

Head south on I-65 to one of the state's best attractions, **Bernheim Arboretum and Research Forest**★★ *(Ky. 245. 502-955-8512. Adm. fee on weekends and holidays).* Established by an immigrant German whiskey distiller, the 14,000-acre Eden holds meticulously maintained gardens, hiking trails, and countless soul-soothing vistas of meadows, lakes, and hills.

Rejoin I-65 and head south to Elizabethtown and **The Schmidt Museum of Coca-Cola Memorabilia**★ *(N on US 31W. 502-737-4000. Adm. fee),* a polished showcase displaying a century of Coke memorabilia.

Hillerich & Bradsby bat factory, Louisville

On the excursion down to cave country, remember to set your watch back an hour as you cross the time zone. First stop, **Kentucky Down Under** *(Ky. 335. 502-786-2634. Adm. fee),* which features a cave tour and an Australian animal park *(April-Oct.).* In the town of **Horse Cave,** the

Kentucky Down Under

Mammoth Cave

Imagine a shallow sea covering middle Kentucky. Then imagine the seabed littered with the crushed shells of billions of tiny creatures. These shells and other sediments, compacted slowly over time, formed the 700-foot-thick layer of limestone that underlies the Mammoth region. The limestone weakened and dissolved under years of rainwater, and the landscape became tunneled by underground rivers, pocked with sinkholes, pitted with caves. Today, 450 feet down, groundwater seepage perpetually creates new cavern passageways, and cave streams knife ever deeper into the earth.

American Cave Museum and Hidden River Cave *(119 E. Main St. 502-786-1466. Adm. fee)* offers a serious introduction to ground-water, karst lands, and cave ecology, plus a tour into the gaping mouth of Hidden River Cave. Groundwater pollution destroyed the cave's fragile ecosystem and closed it for 50 years, but a successful conservation effort has brought back cave fish and tourists.

The real draw around here is, of course, ❹ **Mammoth Cave National Park**★ *(Ky. 70. 502-758-2328. Adm. fee to cave)*, featuring the world's longest network of cavern tunnels—a total of more than 350 known miles. Guided cave tours range from 30-minute strolls to 6.5-hour expeditions; all but the short tours should be booked in advance.

Head back north on I-65, take Ky. 84 over to Hodgenville, and follow signs to the **Abraham Lincoln Birthplace National Historic Site** *(US 31E and Ky. 61. 502-358-3137)*, where a marble and granite memorial contrasts with the primitive backwoods cabin inside, where the 16th U.S. President might have been born. Research has cast doubt on the cabin's authenticity, but the site's quiet, woodsy beauty has been preserved, and trails and exhibits add dimension to a legendary figure. For more insight on the environment that shaped young Lincoln, travel up US 31E to **Lincoln's Boyhood Home** *(US 31E. 502-549-3741. April-Oct.; adm. fee)*, standing in the fertile bottomlands of Knob Creek. Here Abe lived from age 2 to 7 (1811-1816). Again, the rustic cabin is not the original. But it is furnished with pieces donated by descendants of the area's settlers.

Continuing northeast, you travel the same route Lincoln walked to school; the slit of a valley with its sloping pastures, meadows, and small farms probably looks much as it did in Lincoln's time. East of New Haven, the **Trappist-Cistercian Monastery** *(Ky. 247. 502-549-4129)* is a self-supporting community started in 1848 by French monks. Thomas Merton lived and wrote amid these gentle knobs and cleared fields—a perfect setting for a life of prayer, labor, and silence.

Nearby, picturesque ❺ **Bardstown** *(Visitor Center, 107 E. Stephen Foster Ave. 502-348-4877)* is Kentucky's second oldest town. On Court Square, the stone-faced **Old**

Talbott Tavern *(107 W. Stephen Foster Ave. 502-348-3494)* dates from 1779 and has served the likes of Daniel Boone, Jesse James, and King Louis Philippe. Just down the street, the 1819 **St. Joseph's Proto Cathedral** *(US 62W. 502-348-3126)* was the first Roman Catholic cathedral west of the Alleghenies. After admiring the cathedral's fine paintings, step around to the **Oscar Getz Museum of Whiskey History** and **Bardstown Historical Museum**★ *(114 N. 5th St. 502-348-2999. Closed Mon. Nov.-April)* to see a confiscated moonshine still, an exhibit on temperance crusader Carry Nation, and Prohibition-era "medicinal" whiskey bottles.

The area's most popular attraction, **My Old Kentucky Home** *(501 E. Stephen Foster Ave. 502-348-3502. Adm. fee)* is the 1818 federal-style mansion where in 1852 visiting composer Stephen Foster was inspired to write what would become the official state song.

Then it's time for a visit to one of the area's distilleries. Your best bet is **Maker's Mark**★ *(Off Ky. 49 in Loretto. 502-865-2099)*, located in a remote spot 18 miles south of Bardstown. Here you can tour restored buildings where distilling and bottling take place, and soak up the heady aromas of sour mash bourbon aging in white oak casks.

Lincoln's Boyhood Home, near Hodgenville

149

Take US 150 east of Bardstown as it dips and rises through a green countryside of grazing lands and forested hills. Pass through downtown **Springfield,** a quaint old town with an 1816 courthouse, and continue to **Perryville Battlefield State Historic Site** *(County Rd. 1920, 2 miles N of US 150. 606-332-8631. Museum open April-Oct.; adm. fee to museum)*. One of the Civil War's bloodiest battles was fought here on Oct. 8, 1862, resulting in 7,600 casualties and a strategic stalemate.

A little farther east is ❻ **Danville** *(Chamber of Commerce 606-236-7794)*, which boasts an attractive Main Street of 19th-century buildings. The town claims the state's first college (1783) and courthouse (1785). Another first occurred when Dr. Ephraim McDowell removed a 22.5-pound ovarian tumor from a woman in 1809 without anesthesia—the patient quoted the Bible and sang hymns. The site of the operation, the **McDowell House Museum** *(125 S. 2nd St. 606-236-2804. Closed Mon. Nov.- Feb.; adm. fee)*, features the doctor's home, medicinal herb garden, and apothecary.

Now take US 127 north to **Harrodsburg,** Kentucky's oldest town. Founded as a fort on the Wilderness Road in 1774, the town has a number of late 18th-century buildings. Pick up walking and driving tour brochures at the Visitor Center *(103 S. Main. 606-734-2364).* Or, if your time is limited, head straight to **Old Fort Harrod State Park** *(US 127 and Lexington St. 606-734-3314. Closed Mon. and Jan.;*

Shaker Village of Pleasant Hill

adm. fee), a reproduction of the 1774 fort that sheltered the town's first settlers. Part-time residents included George Rogers Clark and Daniel Boone. In the fort's log buildings, craftspeople now demonstrate such pioneer tasks as blacksmithing, woodworking, and quilting. At the same site, the 1830s Greek Revival **Mansion Museum** *(Mid-March–Nov.)* houses nearly 200 pioneer guns and swords, early farm tools and musical instruments, and letters by George Washington and Daniel Boone.

A short distance up US 68 lies a 19th-century commune—the **Shaker Village of Pleasant Hill ★ ★** *(US 68. 606-734-5411. Adm. fee)* was once home to 500 devout Shakers, known for their religious dances, communal property ownership, open confession of sins, celibacy, and seclusion from the world. The community began in 1805 and had disbanded by 1910, but 33 of their buildings still stand. The family dwellings, made of limestone hauled up from the Kentucky River, contain room after spartan room of simple but elegant furniture that reflects their devout lives.

Cumberland Ramble

● **255 miles** ● **2 days** ● **Year-round**

This pleasant drive down Kentucky's midsection covers some of the state's most gorgeous scenery and immerses you in the pioneer heritage of the region. It takes off from Lexington and drops straight south, stopping along the way at a famous abolitionist's mansion, an Appalachian folk arts community, and a frontiersman's house. The route then crosses the Daniel Boone National Forest and enters the Knobs, a region of high, rounded hills.

In Corbin, there's a visit to the original Colonel Sanders restaurant and then an adventurous mountain circuit through Daniel Boone country. Count on seeing plenty of ragged mountains, wooded hollows, gorges, rivers, arches, and steep bluffs. The excursion winds up at lovely Cumberland Falls with, if you're lucky, a look at a rare natural phenomenon—a moonbow.

From Lexington (see Bluegrass–Cave Country drive, p. 144), go south on I-75 and after a few minutes exit east on Ky. 627 to

❶ **Fort Boonesborough State Park** (*Ky. 627. 606-527-3131. Fort open daily April–Labor Day, Wed.-Sun. Labor Day–Oct.; adm. fee to fort*). Tour a reproduction of the fortified village built in 1775 by Daniel Boone and company here beside the Kentucky River. Incited by the British, local Indians constantly attacked the fort. They even captured Boone himself, who managed to escape after a few months. Across the interstate stands **White Hall State Historic Site** (*500 White Hall Shrine Rd. 606-623-9178. Daily April–Labor Day, Wed.-Sun. Labor Day–Oct.; adm. fee*), an

Tobacco barn, east of Berea

1860s mansion owned by one of Kentucky's most colorful characters. Son of a wealthy slaveowner, Cassius Marcellus Clay was a strident abolitionist, a veteran knife fighter and duelist, U.S. minister to Russia, and a founder of the state's Republican Party. At age 84, after his wife of 45 years left him, he married the 15-year-old daughter of a sharecropper, firing a cannon on the posse sent to retrieve the girl.

Back on I-75, zoom down to the foothills, where they begin to show promise of higher mountains. Hidden away here, ❷ **Berea**★ *(Visitor Center, 201 N. Broadway. 606-986-2540)* has maintained its reputation as Kentucky's capital of folk arts and crafts. The small town centers around tuition-free **Berea College** *(606-986-9341)*, founded in 1855 on land donated by Cassius M. Clay; 80 percent of its students come from Appalachia. Around the turn of the century, the college began supporting the region's traditional arts and crafts. Today, Berea's 40-some shops and studios, run by independent artisans, turn out handblown glass, Shaker-style furniture, intricate weavings, and unique pottery.

Start at the **Berea College Appalachian Museum** *(103 Jackson St. 606-986-9341. Closed Jan.; adm. fee)* for an informal introduction to the area's rich folklife. Then take a free tour of the college's craft studios *(Mon.-Fri.)*, which include woodworking, weaving, and broommaking. The college's white-columned **Boone Tavern** *(100 Main St. 606-986-9358)*, an institution since 1909, serves up country ham, spoon bread, and other regional specialties.

A few blocks north, **Churchill Weavers** *(105 Churchill Dr. 606-986-3127. Mon.-Fri.)* also allows free, self-guided tours of its loom house, where some 40 hand-operated wooden looms make decidedly unmodern clacking sounds as they weave fabric the old way.

Fans of country music can catch some of the nation's top performers by heading 11 miles south on I-75 to the **Renfro Valley Entertainment Center** *(March-Dec.; call 606-256-2638 for show times).*

The drive continues south on I-75, climbing out of the valley between high rock walls, then opening up to ever broader views. Exit in London for the ❸ **Levi Jackson Wilderness Road State Park** *(US 25. 606-878-8000. Museum open April-Oct.; adm. fee to museum).* Here you can hike along portions of the Wilderness Road and Boone's Trace, the same trails used by thousands of 18th-century pioneers on their westward treks. The **Mountain Life Museum,** a clutch of relocated and reconstructed log buildings, gives you a good idea of the harsh conditions endured by the state's settlers. Some ended their hard lives in terror: A graveyard holds the remains of 24 people massacred by Indians one night in October 1786.

Now I-75 moves south toward Corbin, where you head east on US 25E. You'll soon see a sign for the **Colonel Harland Sanders Cafe & Museum** *(1 mile S of US 25E. 606-528-2163),* possibly the only fast-food restaurant on the National Register of Historic Places. The megachain began here in the 1940s when the "colonel," after a number of other occupations, settled down to frying chicken for travelers. The restored café is decked out with a 1940 kitchen and motel room, glass display cases, and wood floors. The adjoining, modern KFC looks sterile by comparison.

Berea College Appalachian Museum

As you continue southeast on US 25E, moving up and down the broad slopes of knobs and conical mountains, the land soon takes on the appearance of a giant egg crate. In Pineville, you can pull into ❹ **Pine Mountain State Resort Park** *(Off US 25E, on Ky. 190. 606-337-3066)* and hike up to some fine overlooks of the Cumberland Plateau.

Follow US 25E down to **Cumberland Gap National Historical Park★** *(606-248-2817)* and pop into the Visitor Center for good orientation films about this mountain gateway at the junction of Kentucky, Tennessee, and Virginia. First used by bison, then Indians, explorers, and settlers, the gap allowed access from the eastern seaboard to Kentucky's

153

Bluegrass and beyond. The 20,000-acre park maintains about 50 miles of trails. Drive 4 miles up a steep, switchback road to Pinnacle Overlook for spectacular views of the gap and the serpentine ridge of Cumberland Mountain.

Backtrack just north of Pineville, turn southwest onto Ky. 92, and follow this winding mountain backroad through a landscape of small farms, family-owned grocery stores, and little whitewashed country churches. A sprinkling of houses here and there constitute villages, where old-timers in overalls sit on front porches.

Continue west on Ky. 92 through Williamsburg to **Stearns,** an early 1900s coal company town. At the Visitor Center of **Big South Fork National River and Recreation Area★★** *(Off US 27. 615-879-3625)* pick up literature. The relatively new 110,000-acre preserve straddles Kentucky and Tennessee along the Cumberland Plateau. Heavily mined and logged up until the 1960s, it has since grown wild again, and many old roads are now impassable. A land of natural arches, pinnacles, high cliffs, and rapids, Big South Fork abounds with great hikes, white-water runs, mountain biking, and more.

Housed in the old company headquarters, the **Stearns Museum** *(1 mile W of US 27. 606-376-5730. Daily June-Aug. and Oct., Wed.-Fri. mid-April–May and Sept.; adm. fee)* has interesting displays on mining and lumbering, a moonshiner's still appropriated in 1988, and a jar of "white lightning" for "sniffing, not snorting." Across the street, at the company store and restaurant you can buy locally made crafts or sit at the original marble counter and savor a real milk shake.

For a break from the car, ride the ❺ **Big South Fork Scenic Railway** *(21 S. Main St., off Ky. 92. 606-376-5330 or 800-462-5664. Daily June-Aug. and Oct., Wed.-Sun. mid-April–May and Sept.; fee)* over the mountains and down to **Blue Heron,** an old coal miners' camp that is now part of the recreation area.

You can also drive there, taking Ky. 742 south and west. Just before the road dips down to the Big South Fork, follow signs left for Devil's Jump Overlook and Gorge Overlook—two marvelous views of the Cumberland Plateau threaded by the sinuous river. Down in Blue Heron, you can cross the river on a high footbridge that once served as a coal-tram track. Numerous exhibits detail the mining that went on here from 1937 to 1962, while audio stations give an intimate portrait of life in a place that one woman described as "40 miles from nowhere." You can explore the area further on nature trails and peer into a dark mine tunnel.

Backtrack through Stearns, go north on US 27, then

Hatfield-McCoy Feud

It started around 1880 in Pike County at the West Virginia and Kentucky border. Devil Anse Hatfield of West Virginia and Randall McCoy of Kentucky had fought on opposing sides in the Civil War. Both were tough mountainmen of Scotch and Irish stock, and each had 13 children. The blood sport likely began when a Hatfield boy ran off with a McCoy girl, who came home pregnant. At about the same time, the ownership of a razorback hog was called into question. The location's remoteness and the families' residence in separate states made the case difficult to settle. A morality play of society gone amok, the bitter 15-year quarrel cost some 50 lives.

154

east on Ky. 90. Your final stop, **⑥ Cumberland Falls State Resort Park** ★ *(606-528-4121)* has 17 miles of hiking trails along the Cumberland River. The park's premier feature, the 68-foot-high falls, plunge with such force that mist hangs over the river, creating a rare "moonbow" arc of light on clear, full-moon nights.

Big South Fork National River and Recreation Area

FLORIDA
Florida Tourism Industry and Marketing Corp. General information *904-487-1462.*
Department of Environmental Protection Office of Greenways and Trails *904-488-3701.*
Game and Freshwater Fish Commission Hunting and fishing information *904-488-4676.*
Road Conditions *800-475-0044.*

ALABAMA
Alabama Bureau of Tourism and Travel *334-242-4169 or 800-ALABAMA.*
Department of Conservation and Natural Resources State parks information *334-242-3333.* Division of Game and Fish *334-242-3465.*
Road Conditions *334-242-4378.*

GEORGIA
Georgia Department of Industry, Trade and Tourism *404-656-3550 or 800-VISIT-GA.*
Department of Natural Resources General information *404-656-3530.* Camping reservations *800-864-PARK.* Fishing information *770-918-6418.* Hunting information *770-918-6409.*
Road Conditions *404-656-5267.*

SOUTH CAROLINA
South Carolina Department of Parks, Recreation & Tourism Tourist information *803-734-0122 or 800-364-3634.* Park information *803-734-0156 or 888-88-PARKS.*
Dept. of Wildlife and Freshwater Fisheries Hunting and fishing information *803-734-3888.*

NORTH CAROLINA
North Carolina Department of Travel and Tourism *919-733-4171 or 800-847-4862.*
Department of Environment, Health, and Natural Resources Division of Parks and Recreation *919-733-4181.*
Department of Transportation Ferry service *800-BY-FERRY.*

TENNESSEE
Tennessee Tourism Development General information *615-741-2159.* Booklet and state map *615-741-2158 or 800-836-6200.*
Department of Environment & Conservation Division of State Parks and Recreation *615-532-0001 or 888-867-2757.*
Road Conditions *800-858-6349.*
Wildlife Resources Agency Hunting and fishing information *615-781-6500.*

KENTUCKY
Kentucky Department of Travel Development *502-564-4930 or 800-225-TRIP.*
Department of Fish and Wildlife Resources Hunting and fishing information *502-564-4336.*
Dept. of Parks *502-564-2172 or 800-255-PARK.*
Road Conditions *800-459-7623.*

HOTEL & MOTEL CHAINS
(Accommodations in all states unless otherwise noted)
Best Western Intl. *800-528-1234*
Budget Host *800-BUD-HOST* (except South Carolina and Alabama)

Choice Hotels *800-4-CHOICE*
Clarion Hotels *800-CLARION* (except S.C., Ky., and Ga.)
Comfort Inns *800-228-5150*
Days Inn *800-325-2525*
Doubletree Hotels and Guest Suites *800-222-TREE* (except S.C. and Ala.)
Econo Lodge *800-446-6900*
Embassy Suites *800-362-2779*
Fairfield Inn by Marriott *800-228-2800*
Friendship Inns Hotel *800-453-4511*
Hampton Inn *800-HAMPTON*
Hilton Hotels *800-HILTONS*
Holiday Inns *800-HOLIDAY*
Howard Johnson *800-446-4656*
Hyatt Hotels & Resorts *800-233-1234* (except Alabama)
LRI Loews Hotels *800-223-0888* (except South Carolina and Kentucky)
Motel 6 *800-466-8356*
Quality Inns-Hotels-Suites *800-228-5151*
Radisson Hotels International *800-333-3333*
Ramada Inns *800-2-RAMADA*
Red Roof Inns *800-843-7663*
Ritz-Carlton *800-241-3333* (Florida only)
Sheraton Hotels & Inns *800-325-3535* (except Kentucky)
Super 8 Motels *800-843-1991*
Travelodge Intl., Inc. *800-255-3050*
Utell International *800-223-9868* (except South Carolina and Alabama)
Westin Hotels and Resorts *800-228-3000* (except Kentucky, Tennessee, and Alabama)
Wyndham Hotels and Resorts *800-822-4200* (except Alabama)

ILLUSTRATIONS CREDITS

Photographs in this book are by Raymond Gehman, unless noted: 1, Paul Chesley; 17, Cameron Davidson/Bruce Coleman, Inc.; 26 (upper), Chris Johns, National Geographic Photographer; 29, Stephen Frink; 30, Emory Kristof; 31 (upper), James A. Sugar; 33, Joe McNally; 44, Mike Clemmer; 68, Dana Fineman; 73, David Muench; 93, Bill Terry/Picturesque; 99, David Alan Harvey; 136, Sam Abell, National Geographic Photographer.

NOTES ON AUTHOR AND PHOTOGRAPHER

JOHN M. THOMPSON has covered the South and Midwest for several National Geographic books and was a contributing writer for Michelin's *Florida*. He has lived in North Carolina, Washington, D.C., and Arkansas. Presently he resides in Charlottesville, Virginia, with his wife, Margo, and children, Evan and Claire.

Originally from South Carolina, featured photographer RAYMOND GEHMAN lives in Pennsylvania's Cumberland Valley with his wife and two sons. His recent work includes stories for National Geographic on fire ecology and Banff National Park and photography for books on Canada's Parks and Yellowstone.

157

159

160

Composition for this book by the National
Geographic Society Book Division. Printed
and bound by R.R. Donnelly & Sons, Willard,
Ohio. Color separations by Digital Color
Image, Pensauken, New Jersey. Paper by
Consolidated/Alling & Cory, Willow Grove,
Pennsylvania. Cover printed by Miken Com-
panies, Inc., Cheektowaga, New York.

Library of Congress Cataloging-in-Publication Data

Thompson, John, 1959 Jan. 15-
     National Geographic's driving guides to America.   Florida and the
  Southeast / by John Thompson;   : photographed by Raymond Gehman ; prepared
  by the Book Division, National Geographic Society.
     p.   cm.
     Includes index.
     ISBN 0-7922-3430-8
     1. Florida—Tours. 2. Southern States—Tours. 3. Automobile travel—
  Florida—Guidebooks. 4. Automobile travel—Southern States—Guidebooks.
  I. Gehman, Raymond. II. National Geographic Society (U.S.).   Book Division.
  III. Title. IV. Series.
     F309.3 T49 1997
     917.5904'63—dc21   97-8753
                                                                              CIP

Visit the Society's Web site at http://www.nationalgeographic.com